CONTENTS

About The Author	
Whose Unabomber	3
INDUSTRIAL SOCIETY AND ITS FUTURE	11
Introduction	12
The Psychology Of Modern Leftism	13
Feelings of Inferiority	14
Oversocialization	17
The Power Process	20
Surrogate Activities	21
Autonomy	23
Sources of Social Problems	24
Disruption Of The Power Process In Modern Society	27
How Some People Adjust	32
The Motives of Scientists	35
The Nature of Freedom	37
Some Principles of History	39
Industrial-Technological Society Cannot Be Reformed	42
Restriction Of Freedom Is Unavoidable In Industrial Society	43
The 'Bad' Parts Of Technology Cannot Be Separated From The 'Good' Parts	46
Technology Is A More Powerful Social Force Than The Aspiration For Freedom	48
Simpler Social Problems Have Proved Intractable	52
Revolution is Easier Than Reform	54
Control of Human Behavior	55
Human Race at a Crossroads	61
Human Suffering	63
The Future	65
Strategy	68
Two Kinds of Technology	75
The Danger of Leftism	77
Final Note	82
Notes	83
LETTERS	92

ABOUT THE AUTHOR (from Green Anarchist)

The Unabomber is at the top of America's Most Wanted list, a $1 million reward on his head for 16 bombings since 1978. A specialist team of 150 FBI officers have interviewed over 10,000 suspects and spent $50 million in an unsuccessful attempt to Stop him. They admit he's "very clever" and "a craftsman", exhaustively familiar with explosives 'cookbooks' both commercial and underground, new and old, and individually fashioning the parts of his devices from scrap metal, right down to screws, to make himself more difficult to trace.

He also won celebrity in the US as the "Scarlet Pimpernel of mailbombers" and spectacular publicity for primitivist ideas worldwide during the events that led up to the publication of *Industrial Society & Its Future* in September 1995, forcing even technocrats targeted by him to concede "there's a little bit of the Unabomber in each of us"

The Unabomber's first device, a cigar box with match-head charge and elastic band detonators within, was found in the ear park of the University of Illinois, Chicago, on 2S May 1978. Instead of reaching the professor at New York's Rensselaer Polytechnic Institute it was addressed to, the device was posted back to Northwestern University where it slightly injured a campus cop that became suspicious enough to open it. A second device ignited at Northwestern University almost a year later, 9 May 1979, slightly injuring a student but it was the explosion of a third device in the belly of a Boeing 727 on a domestic flight between Chicago and Washington on 15 November 1979, injuring 12, that got the FBI involved. This third action bought the previous two to light, setting the Feds on their long and fruitless search for Amerika's "lethal Luddite". This new development didn't deter him from posting Percy Wood, president of United Airlines, a book bomb that injured him in Lake Fort. Illinois, On 10 June 1980. The attack on Wood led the FBI to file their elusive serial bomber 'Unabom' – 'Un' standing for 'university' as much as 'United Airlines'.

In his lint 1995 communique to the *New York Times*, the Unabomber conceded planting his next device In a classroom of the University of Utah's Business school on 8 November 1981 was "a mistake". It injured no one.

Two months after a 5 May 1982 pipebombing injured an unidentified academic at Vanderbilt University, Nashville, the Unabomber struck for the first time at the University of California on 2 July 1982. During the national holiday weekend, a parcel bomb was found on the floor of the coffee lounge or the Berkley campuses engineering department. An electronics professor's face and hands were severely damaged as he unwrapped the package, which he mistook for a "measuring instrument". Some firework! Three years later, the Unabomber got right to the belly of the Berkley beast, leaving a parcel bomb in its computer room on 15 May 1985 that cost the maths graduate that opened it the fingers of his right hand.

Leas than a month later, on 13 June 1985, the Boeing Corporation was hit a second time, a bomb being sent to the Washington office but getting intercepted before it could do harm. Less fortunate was the research assistant of a University of Michigan professor. Although sent to his home on 15 November 1985, the assistant was injured opening the parcel for him.

16 bombs in 17 years: The Mail Bombers Trail

Date	Location	What Happened
May 25, 1978	Northwestern Univ Evanston, Ill	Package bomb. 1 injured
May 9, 1979	Northwestern Univ	Bomb in Box. 1 injured
Nov 15, 1979	American Airlines Chicago to Washington	Bomb delivered to unknown location explodes aboard Boeing 727 12 injured
June 10, 1980	Lake Forest, Ill	Package bomb. 1 injured
Oct 8, 1981	Univ of Utah, Salt Lake City	Bomb in classroom No injuries
May 5, 1982	Vanderbilt Univ, Nashville	Pipe Bomb. 1 injured
July 2, 1982	Univ of California at Berkeley	Pipe Bomb. 1 injured
May 15, 1985	Univ of California at Berkeley	Bomb in computer room. 1 serious injury
June 13, 1985	Boeing Company Auburn. Wash.	Package bomb. No injuries
Nov 16, 1985	Ann Arbour. Mich.	Package bomb mail to home of Univ of Mich. professor. 1 Injured
Dec 11, 1985	Sacramento, Calif	Bomb explodes outside a Computer store. 1 death
Feb 20, 1987	Salt Lake City	Bomb outside computer store. 1 injury
June 22, 1993	Tiburon, Calif.	Package bomb, mailed to well known geneticist 1 severe injury
June 24, 1993	Yale Univ. New Haven	Package bomb mailed to professor. 1 severe injury
Dec 10, 1994	North Caldwell, NJ	Package bomb mailed to home of Thomas Mosser NY advertising
April 24, 1995	Sacramento, Calif.	Package bomb mailed to lobbying office of Calif Forestry Assoc. 1 Death

November 1985, the assistant was injured opening the parcel for him. Homan shield tactics or what?

The Unabomber changed tactics too the next month, concealing his next device under wooden boards in the car park of a Sacramento, California, computer store on 11 December 1985. The store manager found the device and, bending to pick it up, had his heart shredded by the ensuing explosion, the first of the Unabomber's targets to die. Clearly encouraged, he tried to repeat this tactic outside a Salt Lake City computer store on 20 February 1987. Again the store manager concerned was injured but someone wearing a hood and big, dark shades the FBI believe may be the Unabamber was spotted in the car park by a woman clerk. This was the closest he ever got to being caught and the FBI themselves admit the standard artist's sketch from the witness description is so "crappy" they can't even decide on his hair colour or estimate his age more accurately than a decade either way decade either way FBI assessment of the Unabomber's motive was equally shakey, consistently visualising him as a 'lone nut' acting out of such unlikely personal motivations as being bump for an airline seat or robbed of employment by a computer automation. Going years without result – perhaps understandably given their methods – the FBI's Unabom task force was eventually disbanded.

There matters might have rested but for the spectacular 1993 World Trade Center bombing by Islamic fundamentalists, apparently offing CIA personnel who regularly parked on the same level as the bomber's truck. Two new Unabomber devices arrived within days on 22 June 1993 at the University of California', Tiburon campus severely injuring a geneticist and on the other side of the continent two days later at Yale University, causing server injury to prominent computer programmer David Gelemter. The Unabomber had not been idle in his 'retirement', the new devices being used upgrading their explosive mix from gunpowder to ammonium nitrate/aluminium filings and swapping elastic detonators for electronic ones. Around this time, the Unabomber made his first approach to the *New York Times*, briefly explaining the bombings were down to the Freedom Club (FC), anti-tech anarchist .

The rapidly reconstituted FBI 'Unabom' task force did nothing to save the life of Thomas Mosser, executive of Burson-Masteller, the ad firm responsible for 'greenwashing' the Exxon Valdez environmental catastrophe. The 'seasonal surprise' was posted to his home at Spen Drive, N. Caldwell, New Jeney on 10 December 1994 and Mosser lost his head over it (Litterallyl) when opened – that'll teach him not to wait until Christmas, eh?

The FBI attribute the Unabomber's last attack to his reaction to militia stooge Tun McVeigh's truck-bombing of Oklahoma's Federal Building. It certainly didn't win his approval: "We Strongly deplore the kind of indiscriminate slaughter that happened in Oklahoma City". Only days afterward, on 24 April 1995, a 10" square box heavily bound with tape arrived at the headquarters of the California Forestry Association, scummy clearcutters and 'wise use' lobbyists rightly despised by Earth Firsters everywhere. Amusingly, staff joked that it might be a bomb and when the corporation' president's' secretary couldn't open it, she did the right thing and passed it on to her boss, even though it was addressed to Gilbert Murray'. predecessor, William Dennison. Many see this misaddressing as evidence this was an express delivery by the Unabomber but Murray or

Dennison, the result was the same whatever - the CFA'. president was successfully assassinated.

This was the last Unabombing to date. Two days after it, FC set forth his terms in a 26 April 1995 letter to the *New York Times*, other US national publications and David Gelenter, the Yale programmer the Unabomber injured in 1993. Thinking it was another bomb, *New York Times* staff passed it on unopened to the FBI - but it came back to them soon enough. Having made good with the deed sixteen times in as many years, the Unabomber now pushed his propaganda as "we feel just now the time is ripe for pushing anti-industrial ideas". He promised to take no further "terrorist" actions if FC's manifesto Industrial Society And Its Future was published. For all their hang-wringing about ethical issues of 'blackmail' and 'giving terrorists the oxygen of publicity supposedly involving in publishing the manifesto, the New York Times was quick enough to publish the Unabomber's communique.

Perhaps out to prove the pen as mighty as the bomb, the Unabomber then sent a series of letters to help concentrate the minds of newspaper editor's subject to his offer. The first reached 1993 Nobel laureates for biology and genetic engineers Richard Roberts of Boston Biotech and Philip Sharpe of Massachusetts Institute of Technology on 8 May 1995, reminding them how much FC disapproved of their research. At the end of June 1995, Los Angeles airport received a letter threatening to blow up an airliner one day, provoking a massively expensive and disruptive security operation, and another the next dismissing the first as a hoax. Unlucky for the FBI, on 2 July 1995, the 13th anniversary of the first Unabombing of Berkeley, another package arrived there from FC. Despite general FBI warnings to all staff, the package was opened by some rent-a-quote psychology professor. He was relieved to find all it contained was a copy of Industrial Society And Its Future manuscript and a list of eminently sane questions, all rather refuting the prof's caricature of the Unabomber as a psycho lacking valid motives.

On 19 September 1995, the newspapers cracked but they'd been cracking way before then. At May 1995's end, a letter the Unabomber had written to *Scientific American* condemning modern science for its "arrogance" made it onto the front cover of *Newsweek*. For weeks following, this world-renown glossy was still printing readers letters praising FC's insights into the crapness of modern life. The most bizarre negotiation was between the Unabomber and *Penthouse*, the Unabomber agreeing to allow FC's manifesto to be published in it but reserving the right to kill one more technocrat subsequently due to *Penthouse's* "inferior quality". Unsurprisingly unhappy with this deal, its editor Bob Guccione then offered the Unabomber a monthly column as an alternative, an offer ultimately not taken up because the *New York Times* and *Washington Post* agreed to joint publication instead. To cover their asses, they had attorney general Janet Reno and FBI director Louis French sprinkle holey water on their decision, insisting they were publishing for reasons of public safety, not journalism. Each paper shouldered $30,000 but for technical reasons the six broadsheet-size pages of *Industrial Society And Its Future* were first run as a supplement in the *Washington Post*. The supplement was deliberately run mid-week to ensure less were produced, a feeble and petulant guesture on the newsmens part Time Warner were good enough to post *Industrial Society And Its Future* on the InterNet and two days later, on the 21 September 1995, the Oakland Tribune also carried the manifesto. This was supposed to be so readers can identify its author from his writing and then grass on him — you wouldn't do that would you? — but in fact *Industrial Society And Its Future* has sparked major debate in the US, for all its reductionism and machismo.

We wish to know no more personal details about the Unabomber than are in the public domain already and have deliberately corrected (but not de-Americanised) spelling in FC's manifesto and communique to reduce the prospect of this publication being used to catch him. We also wish the Unabomber the success and anonymity in his new career as ecoteur.

Editor, *Green Anarchist*,

5 November 1995

WHOSE UNABOMBER?

Technogogues and technopaths we have had with us for some time. The Artificial Intelligence pioneer Marvin Minsky, for instance, was well-known in the early 1980s for his description of the human brain as "a 3 pound computer made of meat". He was featured in the December 1983 issue of *Psychology Today*, occasioning the following letter:

Marvin Minsky:

With the wholly uncritical treatment - nay, giddy embrace - of high technology, even to such excrescences as machine "emotions" which you develop and-promote, *Psychology Today* has at least made it publicly plain what's intended for social life.

Your dehumanizing work is a prime contribution to high tech's accelerating motion towards an ever more artificial, de-individuated, empty landscape.
I believe I am not alone in the opinion that vermin such as you will one day be considered among the world criminals this century hu produced.

In revulsion, John Zerzan

A dozen years later the number of those actively engaged in the desolation of the soul and the murder of nature has probably risen: but i support for the entire framework of such activity has undoubtedly eroded.

Enter Unabomber (he / she / they) with a critique, in acts as well as words, of our sad, perverse, and increasingly bereft technological existence. Unabomber calls for a return to "wild nature" via the "complete and permanent destruction of modern industrial society in every part of the world", and the replacement of that impersonal, unfree, and alienated society by that of small, face-to-face social groupings. He has killed three and wounded 23 in the service of this profoundly radical vision.

There are two somewhat obvious objections to this theory and practice. For one thing, a return to undomesticated anonymous ways of living would not be achieved by the removal of industrialism alone. Such removal would still leave domination of nature, subjugation of women, war, religion, the state, and division of labour, to cite some basic social pathologies. It is civilization itself that must be undone to go where Unabomber wants to go. In other words, the wrong turn for humanity was the Agricultural Revolution, much more fundamentally than the Industrial Revolution.

In terms of practice, the mailing of explosive devices intended for the agents who are engineering the present catastrophe is too random. Children, mail carriers and others could easily be killed. Even if one granted the legitimacy of striking at the high-tech horror show by terrorizing its indispensable architects, collateral harm is not justifiable.

Meanwhile, Unabomber operates in a context of massive psychic immiseration and loss of faith in all of the system's institutions. How many moviegoers, to be more specific, took issue with *Terminator* 2 and it's equating of science and technology with death and destruction? Keay Davidson's "A Rage Against Science" (*San Francisco Examiner*, 30 April 1995) observed that Unabomber's "avowed hatred of science and technological trends reflects growing popular disillusionment with science".

A noteworthy example of the resonance that his sweeping critique of the modern world enjoys is "The Evolution of Despair" by Robert Wright, cover story of *TIME* (or August 28. The long article discusses Unabomber's indictment soberly and sympathetically, in an effort to plumb "the source of our pervasive sense of discontent".

At the same time, not surprisingly, other commentators have sought to minimize the possible impact of such ideas. ""Unabomber Manifesto Not Particularly Unique" is the dismissive summary John Schwartz provided for the August 20 Washington Post. Schwartz found professors who would loftily attest to the unoriginality of fundamental questioning of society, as if anything like that goes on in classrooms. Ellul, Juenger and others with a negative view of technology are far from old hat;

they are unknown, not part of accepted, respected discourse. The cowardice and dishonesty typical of processors and journalists could hardly be more clearly represented.

As easily predicable has been the antipathy to Unabomber-type ideas from the liberal-left. "Unabummer" was Alexander Cockburn's near-hysterical denunciation in *The Nation*, August 28/September 4. This pseudo-critic of US capitalism rants about Unabomber's "homicidal political nuttiness", the fruit of an "'irrational" American anarchist tradition. Cockburn says that Unabomber represents a "rotted - out romanticism of the individual and of nature", that nature is gone forever and we'd better accept it's extinction. In reply to this effort to vilify and marginalize both Unabomber and anarchism, Bob Black points our (unpublished letter to the editor) the world wide resurgence of anarchism and finds the Unabomber expressing:

the best and the predominant thinking in contemporary North American anarchism, which has mostly gotten over the workerism and productivism which it too often used to share with Marxism

In spring 1995, Earth First! spokesperson Judy Bari labelled Unabomber "a sociopath", going on to declare, definitively but mistakenly, that "there is no one in the radical environmental movement who is calling for violence". This is not the place to adequately discuss the politics of radical environmentalism, but Bari's pontificating sounds like the voice of the many anarcho-liberals and anarcho-pacifists who wish to go no further in defence of the wild than tired, ineffective civil disobedience, and who brandish such timid and compromised slogans as "no deforestation without representation".

The summer 1995 issue of *Slingshot*, tabloid of politically correct Berkeley militants, contained a brief editorial trashing Unabomber for creating "'the real danger of government representation" of the radical milieu. The fearless misplaces blame on Unabomber over looks the simple fact that any real blows against the

Megamachine will invite responses from our enemies. The spectre of repression is most effectively banished by doing nothing

For their part "anarchist" of *Love and Rage* (August/Seplember) have also joined the anti-Unabomber leftist chorus. Wayne Price"s "*Is* the Unabomber an Anarchist?" concedes, with Bob Black, that "most anarchists today do not regard the current development of industrial technology as 'progressive' or even neutral, as do Marxists and liberals". But after giving this guarded lip service to the ascendancy of Unabomber-like ideas, Price violently decries Unabomber as a "murderer dragging noble ideas through the mud" and withholds even such political and legal support that he would accord authoritarian leftists targeted by the state. Love and Rage is define by a heavy- handed manipulative organize-the-masses ideology; approaches that are more radical either ignored or condemned by those politicians.

But this selective mini-survey of opposition to Unabomber does not by any means exhaust the range of responses. There are other perspectives, which have mainly, for obvious reasons, been expressed only privately. Some of us, for one thing, have found a glint of hope in the public appearance at last, of a challenge to the fundamentals of a depraved landscape. In distinctions to the widespread feeling that everything outside of the self is beyond our beyond our control, the monopoly of lies has been broken. It might be said that Unabomber's (media) impact is here today, only to be forgotten tomorrow. But at least a few will have been able to understand and remember. The irony, of course, is that lethal bombings were necessary for an alternative to planetary and individual destruction to be allowed to be heard.

The concept of justice should not be overlooked in considering the Unabomber phenomenon. In fact, except for his targets, when have many little Eichmanns who are preparing the Brave New World would have been called to account. Where us any elementary personal responsibility when the planners of our daily and global death march act with complete impunity.

The rolling order rewards such destroyers and tried to polish their image. The May 21 New York Times Magazine's "Unabomber and David Geleniter' summarizes the latter, injured by the a Unabomber bomb at Yale, as a likable computer visionary preparing a "Renaissance of the human spirit". From no other source than the article itself, however, it is clear that Geleniter is helping to user in an new authoritarian dystopia based on all the latest high-tech vistas, like genetic engineering.

Is it unethical to try to stop those whose contributions are bringing an unprecedented assault on life? Or is it unethical to just accept our passive roles in the current zeitgeist of postmodern cynicism and know-nothingism? As a friend in California put it recently, when justice is against the law, only outlaws can effect justice.

The lengthy Unabomber manuscript will go undiscussed here; its strengths and weaknesses deserve separate scrutiny.

These remarks mainly shed light on some of the various, mostly negative commentary rather than directly on their object It is often the case that one can most readily learn about society by watching its ractions, across the spectrum, to those who would challenge it.

Well, I believe In FC/Unabomber — it's all over the country ... his ideas are, as the situationists said, 'in everyone's heads' ; it's just matter of listening to yer own rage

a MidWesterner in the know.

Or as Anne Eisenberg, from Polytechnic University in Brooklyn, admitted, "scratch most people and you'll get a Luddite".

And from the *Boulder Weekly*, Robert Perkinson's, 6 July 1995 column sagely concluded:

Amidst overwhelming madness of unbridled economic growth and postmodern disintegration, is such nostalgia, or even such overwhelming rage, really crazy? For many, especially those who scrape by in unfulfilling jobs and peer longingly towards the stars obscured by beaming street lights, the answer is probably no. And for them, the Unabomber may not be a psychopathic demon. They may wish FC the best of luck.

Autonomous Anarchists Anonymous,
PO Box 11331. Eugene.
Oregon 97440, USA

INDUSTRIAL SOCIETY AND ITS FUTURE

Introduction

1. The Industrial Revolution and its consequences have been a disaster for the human race. They have greatly increased the life-expectancy of those of us who live in "advanced" countries, but they have destabilized society, have made life unfulfilling, have subjected human beings to indignities, have led to widespread psychological suffering (in the Third World to physical suffering as well) and have inflicted severe damage on the natural world. The continued development of technology will worsen the situation. It will certainly subject human beings to greater indignities and inflict greater damage on the natural world, it will probably lead to greater social disruption and psychological suffering, and it may lead to increased physical suffering even in "advanced" countries.

2. The industrial-technological system may survive or it may break down. If it survives, it MAY eventually achieve a low level of physical and psychological suffering, but only after passing through a long and very painful period of adjustment and only at the cost of permanently reducing human beings and many other living organisms to engineered products and mere cogs in the social machine. Furthermore, if the system survives, the consequences will be inevitable: There is no way of reforming or modifying the system so as to prevent it from depriving people of dignity and autonomy.

3. If the system breaks down the consequences will still be very painful. But the bigger the system grows the more disastrous the results of its breakdown will be, so if it is to break down it had best break down sooner rather than later.

4. We therefore advocate a revolution against the industrial system. This revolution may or may not make use of violence; it may be sudden or it may be a relatively gradual process spanning a few decades. We can't predict any of that. But we do outline in a very general way the measures that those who hate the industrial system should take in order to prepare the way for a revolution against that form of society. This is not to be a POLITICAL revolution. Its object will be to overthrow not governments but the economic and technological basis of the present society.

5. In this article we give attention to only some of the negative developments that have grown out of the industrial-technological system. Other such developments we mention only briefly or ignore altogether. This does not mean that we regard these other developments as unimportant. For practical reasons we have to confine our discussion to areas that have received insufficient public attention or in which we have something new to say. For example, since there are well-developed environmental and wilderness movements, we have written very little about environmental degradation or the destruction of wild nature, even though we consider these to be highly important.

THE PSYCHOLOGY OF MODERN LEFTISM

6. Almost everyone will agree that we live in a deeply troubled society. One of the most widespread manifestations of the craziness of our world is leftism, so a discussion of the psychology of leftism can serve as an introduction to the discussion of the problems of modern society in general.

7. But what is leftism? During the first half of the 20th century leftism could have been practically identified with socialism. Today the movement is fragmented and it is not clear who can properly be called a leftist. When we speak of leftists in this article we have in mind mainly socialists, collectivists, "politically correct" types, feminists, gay and disability activists, animal rights activists and the like. But not everyone who is associated with one of these movements is a leftist. What we are trying to get at in discussing leftism is not so much movement or an ideology as a psychological type, or rather a collection of related types. Thus, what we mean by "leftism" will emerge more clearly in the course of our discussion of leftist psychology. (Also, see paragraphs 227-230.)

8. Even so, our conception of leftism will remain a good deal less clear than we would wish, but there doesn't seem to be any remedy for this. All we are trying to do here is indicate in a rough and approximate way the two psychological tendencies that we believe are the main driving force of modern leftism. We by no means claim to be telling the WHOLE truth about leftist psychology. Also, our discussion is meant to apply to modern leftism only. We leave open the question of the extent to which our discussion could be applied to the leftists of the 19th and early 20th centuries.

9. The two psychological tendencies that underlie modern leftism we call "feelings of inferiority" and "oversocialization." Feelings of inferiority are characteristic of modern leftism as a whole, while oversocialization is characteristic only of a certain segment of modern leftism; but this segment is highly influential.

FEELINGS OF INFERIORITY

10. By "feelings of inferiority" we mean not only inferiority feelings in the strict sense but a whole spectrum of related traits; low self-esteem, feelings of powerlessness, depressive tendencies, defeatism, guilt, self-hatred, etc. We argue that modern leftists tend to have some such feelings (possibly more or less repressed) and that these feelings are decisive in determining the direction of modern leftism.

11. When someone interprets as derogatory almost anything that is said about him (or about groups with whom he identifies) we conclude that he has inferiority feelings or low self-esteem. This tendency is pronounced among minority rights activists, whether or not they belong to the minority groups whose rights they defend. They are hypersensitive about the words used to designate minorities and about anything that is said concerning minorities. The terms "negro," "oriental," "handicapped" or "chick" for an African, an Asian, a disabled person or a woman originally had no derogatory connotation. "Broad" and "chick" were merely the feminine equivalents of "guy," "dude" or "fellow." The negative connotations have been attached to these terms by the activists themselves. Some animal rights activists have gone so far as to reject the word "pet" and insist on its replacement by "animal companion." Leftish anthropologists go to great lengths to avoid saying anything about primitive peoples that could conceivably be interpreted as negative. They want to replace the world "primitive" by "nonliterate." They seem almost paranoid about anything that might suggest that any primitive culture is inferior to our own. (We do not mean to imply that primitive cultures ARE inferior to ours. We merely point out the hypersensitivity of leftish anthropologists.)

12. Those who are most sensitive about "politically incorrect" terminology are not the average black ghetto-dweller, Asian immigrant, abused woman or disabled person, but a minority of activists, many of whom do not even belong to any "oppressed" group but come from privileged strata of society. Political correctness has its stronghold among university professors, who have secure employment with comfortable salaries, and the majority of whom are heterosexual white males from middle- to upper-middle-class families.

13. Many leftists have an intense identification with the problems of groups that have an image of being weak (women), defeated (American Indians), repellent (homosexuals) or otherwise inferior. The leftists themselves feel that these groups are inferior. They would never admit to themselves that they have such feelings, but it is precisely because they do see these groups as inferior that they identify with their problems. (We do not mean to suggest that women, Indians, etc. ARE inferior; we are only making a point about leftist psychology.)

14. Feminists are desperately anxious to prove that women are as strong and as capable as men. Clearly they are nagged by a fear that women may NOT be as strong and as capable as men.

15. Leftists tend to hate anything that has an image of being strong, good and successful. They hate America, they hate Western civilization, they hate white males, they hate rationality. The reasons that leftists give for hating the West, etc. clearly do not correspond with their real motives. They SAY they hate the West because it is warlike, imperialistic, sexist, ethnocentric and so forth, but where these same faults appear in socialist countries or in primitive cultures, the leftist finds excuses for them, or at best he GRUDGINGLY admits that they exist; whereas he ENTHUSIASTICALLY points out (and often greatly exaggerates) these faults where they appear in Western civilization. Thus it is clear that these faults are not the leftist's real motive for hating America and the West. He hates America and the West because they are strong and successful.

16. Words like "self-confidence," "self-reliance," "initiative," "enterprise," "optimism," etc., play little role in the liberal and leftist vocabulary. The leftist is anti-individualistic, pro-collectivist. He wants society to solve everyone's problems for them, satisfy everyone's needs for them, take care of them. He is not the sort of person who has an inner sense of confidence in his ability to solve his own problems and satisfy his own needs. The leftist is antagonistic to the concept of competition because, deep inside, he feels like a loser.

17. Art forms that appeal to modern leftish intellectuals tend to focus on sordidness, defeat and despair, or else they take an orgiastic tone, throwing off rational control as if there were no hope of accomplishing anything through rational calculation and all that was left was to immerse oneself in the sensations of the moment.

18. Modern leftish philosophers tend to dismiss reason, science, objective reality and to insist that everything is culturally relative. It is true that one can ask serious questions about the foundations of scientific knowledge and about how, if at all, the concept of objective reality can be defined. But it is obvious that modern leftish philosophers are not simply cool-headed logicians systematically analyzing the foundations of knowledge. They are deeply involved emotionally in their attack on truth and reality. They attack these concepts because of their own psychological needs. For one thing, their attack is an outlet for hostility, and, to the extent that it is successful, it satisfies the drive for power. More importantly, the leftist hates science and rationality because they classify certain beliefs as true (i.e., successful, superior) and other beliefs as false (i.e., failed, inferior). The leftist's feelings of inferiority run so deep that he cannot tolerate any classification of some things as successful or superior and other things as failed or inferior. This also underlies the rejection by many leftists of the concept of mental illness and of the utility of IQ tests. Leftists are antagonistic to genetic explanations of human abilities or behavior because such explanations tend to make some persons appear superior or

inferior to others. Leftists prefer to give society the credit or blame for an individual's ability or lack of it. Thus if a person is "inferior" it is not his fault, but society's, because he has not been brought up properly.

19. The leftist is not typically the kind of person whose feelings of inferiority make him a braggart, an egotist, a bully, a self-promoter, a ruthless competitor. This kind of person has not wholly lost faith in himself. He has a deficit in his sense of power and self-worth, but he can still conceive of himself as having the capacity to be strong, and his efforts to make himself strong produce his unpleasant behavior. [1] But the leftist is too far gone for that. His feelings of inferiority are so ingrained that he cannot conceive of himself as individually strong and valuable. Hence the collectivism of the leftist. He can feel strong only as a member of a large organization or a mass movement with which he identifies himself.

20. Notice the masochistic tendency of leftist tactics. Leftists protest by lying down in front of vehicles, they intentionally provoke police or racists to abuse them, etc. These tactics may often be effective, but many leftists use them not as a means to an end but because they PREFER masochistic tactics. Self-hatred is a leftist trait.

21. Leftists may claim that their activism is motivated by compassion or by moral principles, and moral principle does play a role for the leftist of the oversocialized type. But compassion and moral principle cannot be the main motives for leftist activism. Hostility is too prominent a component of leftist behavior; so is the drive for power. Moreover, much leftist behavior is not rationally calculated to be of benefit to the people whom the leftists claim to be trying to help. For example, if one believes that affirmative action is good for black people, does it make sense to demand affirmative action in hostile or dogmatic terms? Obviously it would be more productive to take a diplomatic and conciliatory approach that would make at least verbal and symbolic concessions to white people who think that affirmative action discriminates against them. But leftist activists do not take such an approach because it would not satisfy their emotional needs. Helping black people is not their real goal. Instead, race problems serve as an excuse for them to express their own hostility and frustrated need for power. In doing so they actually harm black people, because the activists' hostile attitude toward the white majority tends to intensify race hatred.

22. If our society had no social problems at all, the leftists would have to INVENT problems in order to provide themselves with an excuse for making a fuss.

23. We emphasize that the foregoing does not pretend to be an accurate description of everyone who might be considered a leftist. It is only a rough indication of a general tendency of leftism.

OVERSOCIALIZATION

24. Psychologists use the term "socialization" to designate the process by which children are trained to think and act as society demands. A person is said to be well socialized if he believes in and obeys the moral code of his society and fits in well as a functioning part of that society. It may seem senseless to say that many leftists are oversocialized, since the leftist is perceived as a rebel. Nevertheless, the position can be defended. Many leftists are not such rebels as they seem.

25. The moral code of our society is so demanding that no one can think, feel and act in a completely moral way. For example, we are not supposed to hate anyone, yet almost everyone hates somebody at some time or other, whether he admits it to himself or not. Some people are so highly socialized that the attempt to think, feel and act morally imposes a severe burden on them. In order to avoid feelings of guilt, they continually have to deceive themselves about their own motives and find moral explanations for feelings and actions that in reality have a non-moral origin. We use the term "oversocialized" to describe such people. [2]

26. Oversocialization can lead to low self-esteem, a sense of powerlessness, defeatism, guilt, etc. One of the most important means by which our society socializes children is by making them feel ashamed of behavior or speech that is contrary to society's expectations. If this is overdone, or if a particular child is especially susceptible to such feelings, he ends by feeling ashamed of HIMSELF. Moreover the thought and the behavior of the oversocialized person are more restricted by society's expectations than are those of the lightly socialized person. The majority of people engage in a significant amount of naughty behavior. They lie, they commit petty thefts, they break traffic laws, they goof off at work, they hate someone, they say spiteful things or they use some underhanded trick to get ahead of the other guy. The oversocialized person cannot do these things, or if he does do them he generates in himself a sense of shame and self-hatred. The oversocialized person cannot even experience, without guilt, thoughts or feelings that are contrary to the accepted morality; he cannot think "unclean" thoughts. And socialization is not just a matter of morality; we are socialized to conform to many norms of behavior that do not fall under the heading of morality. Thus the oversocialized person is kept on a psychological leash and spends his life running on rails that society has laid down for him. In many oversocialized people this results in a sense of constraint and powerlessness that can be a severe hardship. We suggest that oversocialization is among the more serious cruelties that human beings inflict on one another.

27. We argue that a very important and influential segment of the modern left is oversocialized and that their oversocialization is of great importance in determining the direction of modern leftism. Leftists of the oversocialized type tend to be intellectuals or members of the upper-middle class. Notice that university

intellectuals [3] constitute the most highly socialized segment of our society and also the most left-wing segment.

28. The leftist of the oversocialized type tries to get off his psychological leash and assert his autonomy by rebelling. But usually he is not strong enough to rebel against the most basic values of society. Generally speaking, the goals of today's leftists are NOT in conflict with the accepted morality. On the contrary, the left takes an accepted moral principle, adopts it as its own, and then accuses mainstream society of violating that principle. Examples: racial equality, equality of the sexes, helping poor people, peace as opposed to war, nonviolence generally, freedom of expression, kindness to animals. More fundamentally, the duty of the individual to serve society and the duty of society to take care of the individual. All these have been deeply rooted values of our society (or at least of its middle and upper classes [4] for a long time. These values are explicitly or implicitly expressed or presupposed in most of the material presented to us by the mainstream communications media and the educational system. Leftists, especially those of the oversocialized type, usually do not rebel against these principles but justify their hostility to society by claiming (with some degree of truth) that society is not living up to these principles.

29. Here is an illustration of the way in which the oversocialized leftist shows his real attachment to the conventional attitudes of our society while pretending to be in rebellion against it. Many leftists push for affirmative action, for moving black people into high-prestige jobs, for improved education in black schools and more money for such schools; the way of life of the black "underclass" they regard as a social disgrace. They want to integrate the black man into the system, make him a business executive, a lawyer, a scientist just like upper-middle-class white people. The leftists will reply that the last thing they want is to make the black man into a copy of the white man; instead, they want to preserve African American culture. But in what does this preservation of African American culture consist? It can hardly consist in anything more than eating black-style food, listening to black-style music, wearing black-style clothing and going to a black- style church or mosque. In other words, it can express itself only in superficial matters. In all ESSENTIAL respects most leftists of the oversocialized type want to make the black man conform to white, middle-class ideals. They want to make him study technical subjects, become an executive or a scientist, spend his life climbing the status ladder to prove that black people are as good as white. They want to make black fathers "responsible," they want black gangs to become nonviolent, etc. But these are exactly the values of the industrial-technological system. The system couldn't care less what kind of music a man listens to, what kind of clothes he wears or what religion he believes in as long as he studies in school, holds a respectable job, climbs the status ladder, is a "responsible" parent, is nonviolent and so forth. In effect, however much he may deny it, the oversocialized leftist wants to integrate the black man into the system and make him adopt its values.

30. We certainly do not claim that leftists, even of the oversocialized type, NEVER rebel against the fundamental values of our society. Clearly they sometimes do. Some oversocialized leftists have gone so far as to rebel against one of modern society's most important principles by engaging in physical violence. By their own account, violence is for them a form of "liberation." In other words, by committing violence they break through the psychological restraints that have been trained into them. Because they are oversocialized these restraints have been more confining for them than for others; hence their need to break free of them. But they usually justify their rebellion in terms of mainstream values. If they engage in violence they claim to be fighting against racism or the like.

31. We realize that many objections could be raised to the foregoing thumbnail sketch of leftist psychology. The real situation is complex, and anything like a complete description of it would take several volumes even if the necessary data were available. We claim only to have indicated very roughly the two most important tendencies in the psychology of modern leftism.

32. The problems of the leftist are indicative of the problems of our society as a whole. Low self-esteem, depressive tendencies and defeatism are not restricted to the left. Though they are especially noticeable in the left, they are widespread in our society. And today's society tries to socialize us to a greater extent than any previous society. We are even told by experts how to eat, how to exercise, how to make love, how to raise our kids and so forth.

THE POWER PROCESS

33. Human beings have a need (probably based in biology) for something that we will call the "power process." This is closely related to the need for power (which is widely recognized) but is not quite the same thing. The power process has four elements. The three most clear-cut of these we call goal, effort and attainment of goal. (Everyone needs to have goals whose attainment requires effort, and needs to succeed in attaining at least some of his goals.) The fourth element is more difficult to define and may not be necessary for everyone. We call it autonomy and will discuss it later (paragraphs 42-44).

34. Consider the hypothetical case of a man who can have anything he wants just by wishing for it. Such a man has power, but he will develop serious psychological problems. At first he will have a lot of fun, but by and by he will become acutely bored and demoralized. Eventually he may become clinically depressed. History shows that leisured aristocracies tend to become decadent. This is not true of fighting aristocracies that have to struggle to maintain their power. But leisured, secure aristocracies that have no need to exert themselves usually become bored, hedonistic and demoralized, even though they have power. This shows that power is not enough. One must have goals toward which to exercise one's power.

35. Everyone has goals; if nothing else, to obtain the physical necessities of life: food, water and whatever clothing and shelter are made necessary by the climate. But the leisured aristocrat obtains these things without effort. Hence his boredom and demoralization.

36. Nonattainment of important goals results in death if the goals are physical necessities, and in frustration if nonattainment of the goals is compatible with survival. Consistent failure to attain goals throughout life results in defeatism, low self-esteem or depression.

37. Thus, in order to avoid serious psychological problems, a human being needs goals whose attainment requires effort, and he must have a reasonable rate of success in attaining his goals.

SURROGATE ACTIVITIES

38. But not every leisured aristocrat becomes bored and demoralized. For example, the emperor Hirohito, instead of sinking into decadent hedonism, devoted himself to marine biology, a field in which he became distinguished. When people do not have to exert themselves to satisfy their physical needs they often set up artificial goals for themselves. In many cases they then pursue these goals with the same energy and emotional involvement that they otherwise would have put into the search for physical necessities. Thus the aristocrats of the Roman Empire had their literary pretensions; many European aristocrats a few centuries ago invested tremendous time and energy in hunting, though they certainly didn't need the meat; other aristocracies have competed for status through elaborate displays of wealth; and a few aristocrats, like Hirohito, have turned to science.

39. We use the term "surrogate activity" to designate an activity that is directed toward an artificial goal that people set up for themselves merely in order to have some goal to work toward, or let us say, merely for the sake of the "fulfillment" that they get from pursuing the goal. Here is a rule of thumb for the identification of surrogate activities. Given a person who devotes much time and energy to the pursuit of goal X, ask yourself this: If he had to devote most of his time and energy to satisfying his biological needs, and if that effort required him to use his physical and mental faculties in a varied and interesting way, would he feel seriously deprived because he did not attain goal X? If the answer is no, then the person's pursuit of goal X is a surrogate activity. Hirohito's studies in marine biology clearly constituted a surrogate activity, since it is pretty certain that if Hirohito had had to spend his time working at interesting non-scientific tasks in order to obtain the necessities of life, he would not have felt deprived because he didn't know all about the anatomy and life-cycles of marine animals. On the other hand the pursuit of sex and love (for example) is not a surrogate activity, because most people, even if their existence were otherwise satisfactory, would feel deprived if they passed their lives without ever having a relationship with a member of the opposite sex. (But pursuit of an excessive amount of sex, more than one really needs, can be a surrogate activity.)

40. In modern industrial society only minimal effort is necessary to satisfy one's physical needs. It is enough to go through a training program to acquire some petty technical skill, then come to work on time and exert the very modest effort needed to hold a job. The only requirements are a moderate amount of intelligence and, most of all, simple OBEDIENCE. If one has those, society takes care of one from cradle to grave. (Yes, there is an underclass that cannot take the physical necessities for granted, but we are speaking here of mainstream society.) Thus it is not surprising that modern society is full of surrogate activities. These include scientific work, athletic achievement, humanitarian work, artistic and literary creation, climbing the corporate ladder, acquisition of money and material goods far beyond the point at which they cease to give any additional physical satisfaction, and social activism

when it addresses issues that are not important for the activist personally, as in the case of white activists who work for the rights of nonwhite minorities. These are not always PURE surrogate activities, since for many people they may be motivated in part by needs other than the need to have some goal to pursue. Scientific work may be motivated in part by a drive for prestige, artistic creation by a need to express feelings, militant social activism by hostility. But for most people who pursue them, these activities are in large part surrogate activities. For example, the majority of scientists will probably agree that the "fulfillment" they get from their work is more important than the money and prestige they earn.

41. For many if not most people, surrogate activities are less satisfying than the pursuit of real goals (that is, goals that people would want to attain even if their need for the power process were already fulfilled). One indication of this is the fact that, in many or most cases, people who are deeply involved in surrogate activities are never satisfied, never at rest. Thus the money-maker constantly strives for more and more wealth. The scientist no sooner solves one problem than he moves on to the next. The long-distance runner drives himself to run always farther and faster. Many people who pursue surrogate activities will say that they get far more fulfillment from these activities than they do from the "mundane" business of satisfying their biological needs, but that is because in our society the effort needed to satisfy the biological needs has been reduced to triviality. More importantly, in our society people do not satisfy their biological needs AUTONOMOUSLY but by functioning as parts of an immense social machine. In contrast, people generally have a great deal of autonomy in pursuing their surrogate activities.

AUTONOMY

42. Autonomy as a part of the power process may not be necessary for every individual. But most people need a greater or lesser degree of autonomy in working toward their goals. Their efforts must be undertaken on their own initiative and must be under their own direction and control. Yet most people do not have to exert this initiative, direction and control as single individuals. It is usually enough to act as a member of a SMALL group. Thus if half a dozen people discuss a goal among themselves and make a successful joint effort to attain that goal, their need for the power process will be served. But if they work under rigid orders handed down from above that leave them no room for autonomous decision and initiative, then their need for the power process will not be served. The same is true when decisions are made on a collective basis if the group making the collective decision is so large that the role of each individual is insignificant. [5]

43. It is true that some individuals seem to have little need for autonomy. Either their drive for power is weak or they satisfy it by identifying themselves with some powerful organization to which they belong. And then there are unthinking, animal types who seem to be satisfied with a purely physical sense of power (the good combat soldier, who gets his sense of power by developing fighting skills that he is quite content to use in blind obedience to his superiors).

44. But for most people it is through the power process—having a goal, making an AUTONOMOUS effort and attaining the goal—that self-esteem, self-confidence and a sense of power are acquired. When one does not have adequate opportunity to go through the power process the consequences are (depending on the individual and on the way the power process is disrupted) boredom, demoralization, low self-esteem, inferiority feelings, defeatism, depression, anxiety, guilt, frustration, hostility, spouse or child abuse, insatiable hedonism, abnormal sexual behavior, sleep disorders, eating disorders, etc. [6]

SOURCES OF SOCIAL PROBLEMS

45. Any of the foregoing symptoms can occur in any society, but in modern industrial society they are present on a massive scale. We aren't the first to mention that the world today seems to be going crazy. This sort of thing is not normal for human societies. There is good reason to believe that primitive man suffered from less stress and frustration and was better satisfied with his way of life than modern man is. It is true that not all was sweetness and light in primitive societies. Abuse of women was common among the Australian aborigines, transexuality was fairly common among some of the American Indian tribes. But it does appear that GENERALLY SPEAKING the kinds of problems that we have listed in the preceding paragraph were far less common among primitive peoples than they are in modern society.

46. We attribute the social and psychological problems of modern society to the fact that that society requires people to live under conditions radically different from those under which the human race evolved and to behave in ways that conflict with the patterns of behavior that the human race developed while living under the earlier conditions. It is clear from what we have already written that we consider lack of opportunity to properly experience the power process as the most important of the abnormal conditions to which modern society subjects people. But it is not the only one. Before dealing with disruption of the power process as a source of social problems we will discuss some of the other sources.

47. Among the abnormal conditions present in modern industrial society are excessive density of population, isolation of man from nature, excessive rapidity of social change and the breakdown of natural small-scale communities such as the extended family, the village or the tribe.

48. It is well known that crowding increases stress and aggression. The degree of crowding that exists today and the isolation of man from nature are consequences of technological progress. All pre-industrial societies were predominantly rural. The Industrial Revolution vastly increased the size of cities and the proportion of the population that lives in them, and modern agricultural technology has made it possible for the Earth to support a far denser population than it ever did before. (Also, technology exacerbates the effects of crowding because it puts increased disruptive powers in people's hands. For example, a variety of noise- making devices: power mowers, radios, motorcycles, etc. If the use of these devices is unrestricted, people who want peace and quiet are frustrated by the noise. If their use is restricted, people who use the devices are frustrated by the regulations. But if these machines had never been invented there would have been no conflict and no frustration generated by them.)

49. For primitive societies the natural world (which usually changes only slowly) provided a stable framework and therefore a sense of security. In the modern world it is human society that dominates nature rather than the other way around, and modern society changes very rapidly owing to technological change. Thus there is no stable framework.

50. The conservatives are fools: They whine about the decay of traditional values, yet they enthusiastically support technological progress and economic growth. Apparently it never occurs to them that you can't make rapid, drastic changes in the technology and the economy of a society without causing rapid changes in all other aspects of the society as well, and that such rapid changes inevitably break down traditional values.

51. The breakdown of traditional values to some extent implies the breakdown of the bonds that hold together traditional small-scale social groups. The disintegration of small-scale social groups is also promoted by the fact that modern conditions often require or tempt individuals to move to new locations, separating themselves from their communities. Beyond that, a technological society HAS TO weaken family ties and local communities if it is to function efficiently. In modern society an individual's loyalty must be first to the system and only secondarily to a small-scale community, because if the internal loyalties of small-scale communities were stronger than loyalty to the system, such communities would pursue their own advantage at the expense of the system.

52. Suppose that a public official or a corporation executive appoints his cousin, his friend or his co- religionist to a position rather than appointing the person best qualified for the job. He has permitted personal loyalty to supersede his loyalty to the system, and that is "nepotism" or "discrimination," both of which are terrible sins in modern society. Would-be industrial societies that have done a poor job of subordinating personal or local loyalties to loyalty to the system are usually very inefficient. (Look at Latin America.) Thus an advanced industrial society can tolerate only those small-scale communities that are emasculated, tamed and made into tools of the system. [7]

53. Crowding, rapid change and the breakdown of communities have been widely recognized as sources of social problems. But we do not believe they are enough to account for the extent of the problems that are seen today.

54. A few pre-industrial cities were very large and crowded, yet their inhabitants do not seem to have suffered from psychological problems to the same extent as modern man. In America today there still are uncrowded rural areas, and we find there the same problems as in urban areas, though the problems tend to be less acute in the rural areas. Thus crowding does not seem to be the decisive factor.

55. On the growing edge of the American frontier during the 19th century, the mobility of the population probably broke down extended families and small-scale social groups to at least the same extent as these are broken down today. In fact, many nuclear families lived by choice in such isolation, having no neighbors within several miles, that they belonged to no community at all, yet they do not seem to have developed problems as a result.

56. Furthermore, change in American frontier society was very rapid and deep. A man might be born and raised in a log cabin, outside the reach of law and order and fed largely on wild meat; and by the time he arrived at old age he might be working at a regular job and living in an ordered community with effective law enforcement. This was a deeper change than that which typically occurs in the life of a modern individual, yet it does not seem to have led to psychological problems. In fact, 19th century American society had an optimistic and self-confident tone, quite unlike that of today's society. [8]

57. The difference, we argue, is that modern man has the sense (largely justified) that change is IMPOSED on him, whereas the 19th century frontiersman had the sense (also largely justified) that he created change himself, by his own choice. Thus a pioneer settled on a piece of land of his own choosing and made it into a farm through his own effort. In those days an entire county might have only a couple of hundred inhabitants and was a far more isolated and autonomous entity than a modern county is. Hence the pioneer farmer participated as a member of a relatively small group in the creation of a new, ordered community. One may well question whether the creation of this community was an improvement, but at any rate it satisfied the pioneer's need for the power process.

58. It would be possible to give other examples of societies in which there has been rapid change and/or lack of close community ties without the kind of massive behavioral aberration that is seen in today's industrial society. We contend that the most important cause of social and psychological problems in modern society is the fact that people have insufficient opportunity to go through the power process in a normal way. We don't mean to say that modern society is the only one in which the power process has been disrupted. Probably most if not all civilized societies have interfered with the power process to a greater or lesser extent. But in modern industrial society the problem has become particularly acute. Leftism, at least in its recent (mid- to late-20th century) form, is in part a symptom of deprivation with respect to the power process.

DISRUPTION OF THE POWER
PROCESS IN MODERN SOCIETY

59. We divide human drives into three groups: (1) those drives that can be satisfied with minimal effort; (2) those that can be satisfied but only at the cost of serious effort; (3) those that cannot be adequately satisfied no matter how much effort one makes. The power process is the process of satisfying the drives of the second group. The more drives there are in the third group, the more there is frustration, anger, eventually defeatism, depression, etc.

60. In modern industrial society natural human drives tend to be pushed into the first and third groups, and the second group tends to consist increasingly of artificially created drives.

61. In primitive societies, physical necessities generally fall into group 2: They can be obtained, but only at the cost of serious effort. But modern society tends to guaranty the physical necessities to everyone [9] in exchange for only minimal effort, hence physical needs are pushed into group 1. (There may be disagreement about whether the effort needed to hold a job is "minimal"; but usually, in lower- to middle-level jobs, whatever effort is required is merely that of OBEDIENCE. You sit or stand where you are told to sit or stand and do what you are told to do in the way you are told to do it. Seldom do you have to exert yourself seriously, and in any case you have hardly any autonomy in work, so that the need for the power process is not well served.)

62. Social needs, such as sex, love and status, often remain in group 2 in modern society, depending on the situation of the individual. [10] But, except for people who have a particularly strong drive for status, the effort required to fulfill the social drives is insufficient to satisfy adequately the need for the power process.

63. So certain artificial needs have been created that fall into group 2, hence serve the need for the power process. Advertising and marketing techniques have been developed that make many people feel they need things that their grandparents never desired or even dreamed of. It requires serious effort to earn enough money to satisfy these artificial needs, hence they fall into group 2. (But see paragraphs 80-82.) Modern man must satisfy his need for the power process largely through pursuit of the artificial needs created by the advertising and marketing industry [11], and through surrogate activities.

64. It seems that for many people, maybe the majority, these artificial forms of the power process are insufficient. A theme that appears repeatedly in the writings of

the social critics of the second half of the 20th century is the sense of purposelessness that afflicts many people in modern society. (This purposelessness is often called by other names such as "anomie" or "middle-class vacuity.") We suggest that the so-called "identity crisis" is actually a search for a sense of purpose, often for commitment to a suitable surrogate activity. It may be that existentialism is in large part a response to the purposelessness of modern life. [12] Very widespread in modern society is the search for "fulfillment." But we think that for the majority of people an activity whose main goal is fulfillment (that is, a surrogate activity) does not bring completely satisfactory fulfillment. In other words, it does not fully satisfy the need for the power process. (See paragraph 41.) That need can be fully satisfied only through activities that have some external goal, such as physical necessities, sex, love, status, revenge, etc.

65. Moreover, where goals are pursued through earning money, climbing the status ladder or functioning as part of the system in some other way, most people are not in a position to pursue their goals AUTONOMOUSLY. Most workers are someone else's employee and, as we pointed out in paragraph 61, must spend their days doing what they are told to do in the way they are told to do it. Even people who are in business for themselves have only limited autonomy. It is a chronic complaint of small-business persons and entrepreneurs that their hands are tied by excessive government regulation. Some of these regulations are doubtless unnecessary, but for the most part government regulations are essential and inevitable parts of our extremely complex society. A large portion of small business today operates on the franchise system. It was reported in the Wall Street Journal a few years ago that many of the franchise-granting companies require applicants for franchises to take a personality test that is designed to EXCLUDE those who have creativity and initiative, because such persons are not sufficiently docile to go along obediently with the franchise system. This excludes from small business many of the people who most need autonomy.

66. Today people live more by virtue of what the system does FOR them or TO them than by virtue of what they do for themselves. And what they do for themselves is done more and more along channels laid down by the system. Opportunities tend to be those that the system provides, the opportunities must be exploited in accord with rules and regulations [13], and techniques prescribed by experts must be followed if there is to be a chance of success.

67. Thus the power process is disrupted in our society through a deficiency of real goals and a deficiency of autonomy in the pursuit of goals. But it is also disrupted because of those human drives that fall into group 3: the drives that one cannot adequately satisfy no matter how much effort one makes. One of these drives is the need for security. Our lives depend on decisions made by other people; we have no control over these decisions and usually we do not even know the people who make them. ("We live in a world in which relatively few people—maybe 500 or 1,000—make the important decisions"—Philip B. Heymann of Harvard Law School, quoted by Anthony Lewis, New York Times, April 21, 1995.) Our lives depend on whether safety standards at a nuclear power plant are properly maintained; on how much pesticide

is allowed to get into our food or how much pollution into our air; on how skillful (or incompetent) our doctor is; whether we lose or get a job may depend on decisions made by government economists or corporation executives; and so forth. Most individuals are not in a position to secure themselves against these threats to more [than] a very limited extent. The individual's search for security is therefore frustrated, which leads to a sense of powerlessness.

68. It may be objected that primitive man is physically less secure than modern man, as is shown by his shorter life expectancy; hence modern man suffers from less, not more than the amount of insecurity that is normal for human beings. But psychological security does not closely correspond with physical security. What makes us FEEL secure is not so much objective security as a sense of confidence in our ability to take care of ourselves. Primitive man, threatened by a fierce animal or by hunger, can fight in self-defense or travel in search of food. He has no certainty of success in these efforts, but he is by no means helpless against the things that threaten him. The modern individual on the other hand is threatened by many things against which he is helpless: nuclear accidents, carcinogens in food, environmental pollution, war, increasing taxes, invasion of his privacy by large organizations, nationwide social or economic phenomena that may disrupt his way of life.

69. It is true that primitive man is powerless against some of the things that threaten him; disease for example. But he can accept the risk of disease stoically. It is part of the nature of things, it is no one's fault, unless it is the fault of some imaginary, impersonal demon. But threats to the modern individual tend to be MAN-MADE. They are not the results of chance but are IMPOSED on him by other persons whose decisions he, as an individual, is unable to influence. Consequently he feels frustrated, humiliated and angry.

70. Thus primitive man for the most part has his security in his own hands (either as an individual or as a member of a SMALL group) whereas the security of modern man is in the hands of persons or organizations that are too remote or too large for him to be able personally to influence them. So modern man's drive for security tends to fall into groups 1 and 3; in some areas (food, shelter etc.) his security is assured at the cost of only trivial effort, whereas in other areas he CANNOT attain security. (The foregoing greatly simplifies the real situation, but it does indicate in a rough, general way how the condition of modern man differs from that of primitive man.)

71. People have many transitory drives or impulses that are necessarily frustrated in modern life, hence fall into group 3. One may become angry, but modern society cannot permit fighting. In many situations it does not even permit verbal aggression. When going somewhere one may be in a hurry, or one may be in a mood to travel slowly, but one generally has no choice but to move with the flow of traffic and obey the traffic signals. One may want to do one's work in a different way, but usually one can work only according to the rules laid down by one's employer. In many other ways as well, modern man is strapped down by a network of rules and regulations (explicit

or implicit) that frustrate many of his impulses and thus interfere with the power process. Most of these regulations cannot be dispensed with, because they are necessary for the functioning of industrial society.

72. Modern society is in certain respects extremely permissive. In matters that are irrelevant to the functioning of the system we can generally do what we please. We can believe in any religion we like (as long as it does not encourage behavior that is dangerous to the system). We can go to bed with anyone we like (as long as we practice "safe sex"). We can do anything we like as long as it is UNIMPORTANT. But in all IMPORTANT matters the system tends increasingly to regulate our behavior.

73. Behavior is regulated not only through explicit rules and not only by the government. Control is often exercised through indirect coercion or through psychological pressure or manipulation, and by organizations other than the government, or by the system as a whole. Most large organizations use some form of propaganda [14] to manipulate public attitudes or behavior. Propaganda is not limited to "commercials" and advertisements, and sometimes it is not even consciously intended as propaganda by the people who make it. For instance, the content of entertainment programming is a powerful form of propaganda. An example of indirect coercion: There is no law that says we have to go to work every day and follow our employer's orders. Legally there is nothing to prevent us from going to live in the wild like primitive people or from going into business for ourselves. But in practice there is very little wild country left, and there is room in the economy for only a limited number of small business owners. Hence most of us can survive only as someone else's employee.

74. We suggest that modern man's obsession with longevity, and with maintaining physical vigor and sexual attractiveness to an advanced age, is a symptom of unfulfillment resulting from deprivation with respect to the power process. The "midlife crisis" also is such a symptom. So is the lack of interest in having children that is fairly common in modern society but almost unheard-of in primitive societies.

75. In primitive societies life is a succession of stages. The needs and purposes of one stage having been fulfilled, there is no particular reluctance about passing on to the next stage. A young man goes through the power process by becoming a hunter, hunting not for sport or for fulfillment but to get meat that is necessary for food. (In young women the process is more complex, with greater emphasis on social power; we won't discuss that here.) This phase having been successfully passed through, the young man has no reluctance about settling down to the responsibilities of raising a family. (In contrast, some modern people indefinitely postpone having children because they are too busy seeking some kind of "fulfillment." We suggest that the fulfillment they need is adequate experience of the power process—with real goals instead of the artificial goals of surrogate activities.) Again, having successfully raised his children, going through the power process by providing them with the physical necessities, the primitive man feels that his work is done and he is prepared to accept old age (if he survives that long) and death. Many modern people, on the

other hand, are disturbed by the prospect of physical deterioration and death, as is shown by the amount of effort they expend trying to maintain their physical condition, appearance and health. We argue that this is due to unfulfillment resulting from the fact that they have never put their physical powers to any practical use, have never gone through the power process using their bodies in a serious way. It is not the primitive man, who has used his body daily for practical purposes, who fears the deterioration of age, but the modern man, who has never had a practical use for his body beyond walking from his car to his house. It is the man whose need for the power process has been satisfied during his life who is best prepared to accept the end of that life.

76. In response to the arguments of this section someone will say, "Society must find a way to give people the opportunity to go through the power process." For such people the value of the opportunity is destroyed by the very fact that society gives it to them. What they need is to find or make their own opportunities. As long as the system GIVES them their opportunities it still has them on a leash. To attain autonomy they must get off that leash.

HOW SOME PEOPLE ADJUST

77. Not everyone in industrial-technological society suffers from psychological problems. Some people even profess to be quite satisfied with society as it is. We now discuss some of the reasons why people differ so greatly in their response to modern society.

78. First, there doubtless are differences in the strength of the drive for power. Individuals with a weak drive for power may have relatively little need to go through the power process, or at least relatively little need for autonomy in the power process. These are docile types who would have been happy as plantation darkies in the Old South. (We don't mean to sneer at the "plantation darkies" of the Old South. To their credit, most of the slaves were NOT content with their servitude. We do sneer at people who ARE content with servitude.)

79. Some people may have some exceptional drive, in pursuing which they satisfy their need for the power process. For example, those who have an unusually strong drive for social status may spend their whole lives climbing the status ladder without ever getting bored with that game.

80. People vary in their susceptibility to advertising and marketing techniques. Some are so susceptible that, even if they make a great deal of money, they cannot satisfy their constant craving for the the shiny new toys that the marketing industry dangles before their eyes. So they always feel hard-pressed financially even if their income is large, and their cravings are frustrated.

81. Some people have low susceptibility to advertising and marketing techniques. These are the people who aren't interested in money. Material acquisition does not serve their need for the power process.

82. People who have medium susceptibility to advertising and marketing techniques are able to earn enough money to satisfy their craving for goods and services, but only at the cost of serious effort (putting in overtime, taking a second job, earning promotions, etc.). Thus material acquisition serves their need for the power process. But it does not necessarily follow that their need is fully satisfied. They may have insufficient autonomy in the power process (their work may consist of following orders) and some of their drives may be frustrated (e.g., security, aggression). (We are guilty of oversimplification in paragraphs 80- 82 because we have assumed that the desire for material acquisition is entirely a creation of the advertising and marketing industry. Of course it's not that simple. [11]

83. Some people partly satisfy their need for power by identifying themselves with a powerful organization or mass movement. An individual lacking goals or power joins a movement or an organization, adopts its goals as his own, then works toward those goals. When some of the goals are attained, the individual, even though his personal efforts have played only an insignificant part in the attainment of the goals, feels (through his identification with the movement or organization) as if he had gone through the power process. This phenomenon was exploited by the fascists, nazis and communists. Our society uses it too, though less crudely. Example: Manuel Noriega was an irritant to the U.S. (goal: punish Noriega). The U.S. invaded Panama (effort) and punished Noriega (attainment of goal). Thus the U.S. went through the power process and many Americans, because of their identification with the U.S., experienced the power process vicariously. Hence the widespread public approval of the Panama invasion; it gave people a sense of power. [15] We see the same phenomenon in armies, corporations, political parties, humanitarian organizations, religious or ideological movements. In particular, leftist movements tend to attract people who are seeking to satisfy their need for power. But for most people identification with a large organization or a mass movement does not fully satisfy the need for power.

84. Another way in which people satisfy their need for the power process is through surrogate activities. As we explained in paragraphs 38-40, a surrogate activity is an activity that is directed toward an artificial goal that the individual pursues for the sake of the "fulfillment" that he gets from pursuing the goal, not because he needs to attain the goal itself. For instance, there is no practical motive for building enormous muscles, hitting a little ball into a hole or acquiring a complete series of postage stamps. Yet many people in our society devote themselves with passion to bodybuilding, golf or stamp-collecting. Some people are more "other-directed" than others, and therefore will more readily attach importance to a surrogate activity simply because the people around them treat it as important or because society tells them it is important. That is why some people get very serious about essentially trivial activities such as sports, or bridge, or chess, or arcane scholarly pursuits, whereas others who are more clear-sighted never see these things as anything but the surrogate activities that they are, and consequently never attach enough importance to them to satisfy their need for the power process in that way. It only remains to point out that in many cases a person's way of earning a living is also a surrogate activity. Not a PURE surrogate activity, since part of the motive for the activity is to gain the physical necessities and (for some people) social status and the luxuries that advertising makes them want. But many people put into their work far more effort than is necessary to earn whatever money and status they require, and this extra effort constitutes a surrogate activity. This extra effort, together with the emotional investment that accompanies it, is one of the most potent forces acting toward the continual development and perfecting of the system, with negative consequences for individual freedom (see paragraph 131). Especially, for the most creative scientists and engineers, work tends to be largely a surrogate activity. This point is so important that it deserves a separate discussion, which we shall give in a moment (paragraphs 87-92).

85. In this section we have explained how many people in modern society do satisfy their need for the power process to a greater or lesser extent. But we think that for the majority of people the need for the power process is not fully satisfied. In the first place, those who have an insatiable drive for status, or who get firmly "hooked" on a surrogate activity, or who identify strongly enough with a movement or organization to satisfy their need for power in that way, are exceptional personalities. Others are not fully satisfied with surrogate activities or by identification with an organization (see paragraphs 41, 64). In the second place, too much control is imposed by the system through explicit regulation or through socialization, which results in a deficiency of autonomy, and in frustration due to the impossibility of attaining certain goals and the necessity of restraining too many impulses.

86. But even if most people in industrial-technological society were well satisfied, we (FC) would still be opposed to that form of society, because (among other reasons) we consider it demeaning to fulfill one's need for the power process through surrogate activities or through identification with an organization, rather than through pursuit of real goals.

THE MOTIVES OF SCIENTISTS

87. Science and technology provide the most important examples of surrogate activities. Some scientists claim that they are motivated by "curiosity" or by a desire to "benefit humanity." But it is easy to see that neither of these can be the principal motive of most scientists. As for "curiosity," that notion is simply absurd. Most scientists work on highly specialized problems that are not the object of any normal curiosity. For example, is an astronomer, a mathematician or an entomologist curious about the properties of isopropyltrimethylmethane? Of course not. Only a chemist is curious about such a thing, and he is curious about it only because chemistry is his surrogate activity. Is the chemist curious about the appropriate classification of a new species of beetle? No. That question is of interest only to the entomologist, and he is interested in it only because entomology is his surrogate activity. If the chemist and the entomologist had to exert themselves seriously to obtain the physical necessities, and if that effort exercised their abilities in an interesting way but in some nonscientific pursuit, then they wouldn't give a damn about isopropyltrimethylmethane or the classification of beetles. Suppose that lack of funds for postgraduate education had led the chemist to become an insurance broker instead of a chemist. In that case he would have been very interested in insurance matters but would have cared nothing about isopropyltrimethylmethane. In any case it is not normal to put into the satisfaction of mere curiosity the amount of time and effort that scientists put into their work. The "curiosity" explanation for the scientists' motive just doesn't stand up.

88. The "benefit of humanity" explanation doesn't work any better. Some scientific work has no conceivable relation to the welfare of the human race—most of archaeology or comparative linguistics for example. Some other areas of science present obviously dangerous possibilities. Yet scientists in these areas are just as enthusiastic about their work as those who develop vaccines or study air pollution. Consider the case of Dr. Edward Teller, who had an obvious emotional involvement in promoting nuclear power plants. Did this involvement stem from a desire to benefit humanity? If so, then why didn't Dr. Teller get emotional about other "humanitarian" causes? If he was such a humanitarian then why did he help to develop the H-bomb? As with many other scientific achievements, it is very much open to question whether nuclear power plants actually do benefit humanity. Does the cheap electricity outweigh the accumulating waste and the risk of accidents? Dr. Teller saw only one side of the question. Clearly his emotional involvement with nuclear power arose not from a desire to "benefit humanity" but from a personal fulfillment he got from his work and from seeing it put to practical use.

89. The same is true of scientists generally. With possible rare exceptions, their motive is neither curiosity nor a desire to benefit humanity but the need to go through the power process: to have a goal (a scientific problem to solve), to make an effort (research) and to attain the goal (solution of the problem.) Science is a

surrogate activity because scientists work mainly for the fulfillment they get out of the work itself.

90. Of course, it's not that simple. Other motives do play a role for many scientists. Money and status for example. Some scientists may be persons of the type who have an insatiable drive for status (see paragraph 79) and this may provide much of the motivation for their work. No doubt the majority of scientists, like the majority of the general population, are more or less susceptible to advertising and marketing techniques and need money to satisfy their craving for goods and services. Thus science is not a PURE surrogate activity. But it is in large part a surrogate activity.

91. Also, science and technology constitute a power mass movement, and many scientists gratify their need for power through identification with this mass movement (see paragraph 83).

92. Thus science marches on blindly, without regard to the real welfare of the human race or to any other standard, obedient only to the psychological needs of the scientists and of the government officials and corporation executives who provide the funds for research.

THE NATURE OF FREEDOM

93. We are going to argue that industrial-technological society cannot be reformed in such a way as to prevent it from progressively narrowing the sphere of human freedom. But, because "freedom" is a word that can be interpreted in many ways, we must first make clear what kind of freedom we are concerned with.

94. By "freedom" we mean the opportunity to go through the power process, with real goals not the artificial goals of surrogate activities, and without interference, manipulation or supervision from anyone, especially from any large organization. Freedom means being in control (either as an individual or as a member of a SMALL group) of the life-and-death issues of one's existence; food, clothing, shelter and defense against whatever threats there may be in one's environment. Freedom means having power; not the power to control other people but the power to control the circumstances of one's own life. One does not have freedom if anyone else (especially a large organization) has power over one, no matter how benevolently, tolerantly and permissively that power may be exercised. It is important not to confuse freedom with mere permissiveness (see paragraph 72).

95. It is said that we live in a free society because we have a certain number of constitutionally guaranteed rights. But these are not as important as they seem. The degree of personal freedom that exists in a society is determined more by the economic and technological structure of the society than by its laws or its form of government. [16] Most of the Indian nations of New England were monarchies, and many of the cities of the Italian Renaissance were controlled by dictators. But in reading about these societies one gets the impression that they allowed far more personal freedom than our society does. In part this was because they lacked efficient mechanisms for enforcing the ruler's will: There were no modern, well-organized police forces, no rapid long-distance communications, no surveillance cameras, no dossiers of information about the lives of average citizens. Hence it was relatively easy to evade control.

96. As for our constitutional rights, consider for example that of freedom of the press. We certainly don't mean to knock that right; it is very important tool for limiting concentration of political power and for keeping those who do have political power in line by publicly exposing any misbehavior on their part. But freedom of the press is of very little use to the average citizen as an individual. The mass media are mostly under the control of large organizations that are integrated into the system. Anyone who has a little money can have something printed, or can distribute it on the Internet or in some such way, but what he has to say will be swamped by the vast volume of material put out by the media, hence it will have no practical effect. To make an impression on society with words is therefore almost impossible for most individuals and small groups. Take us (FC) for example. If we had never done anything

violent and had submitted the present writings to a publisher, they probably would not have been accepted. If they had been been accepted and published, they probably would not have attracted many readers, because it's more fun to watch the entertainment put out by the media than to read a sober essay. Even if these writings had had many readers, most of these readers would soon have forgotten what they had read as their minds were flooded by the mass of material to which the media expose them. In order to get our message before the public with some chance of making a lasting impression, we've had to kill people.

97. Constitutional rights are useful up to a point, but they do not serve to guarantee much more than what might be called the bourgeois conception of freedom. According to the bourgeois conception, a "free" man is essentially an element of a social machine and has only a certain set of prescribed and delimited freedoms; freedoms that are designed to serve the needs of the social machine more than those of the individual. Thus the bourgeois's "free" man has economic freedom because that promotes growth and progress; he has freedom of the press because public criticism restrains misbehavior by political leaders; he has a right to a fair trial because imprisonment at the whim of the powerful would be bad for the system. This was clearly the attitude of Simon Bolivar. To him, people deserved liberty only if they used it to promote progress (progress as conceived by the bourgeois). Other bourgeois thinkers have taken a similar view of freedom as a mere means to collective ends. Chester C. Tan, "Chinese Political Thought in the Twentieth Century," page 202, explains the philosophy of the Kuomintang leader Hu Han-min: "An individual is granted rights because he is a member of society and his community life requires such rights. By community Hu meant the whole society of the nation." And on page 259 Tan states that according to Carsum Chang (Chang Chun-mai, head of the State Socialist Party in China) freedom had to be used in the interest of the state and of the people as a whole. But what kind of freedom does one have if one can use it only as someone else prescribes? FC's conception of freedom is not that of Bolivar, Hu, Chang or other bourgeois theorists. The trouble with such theorists is that they have made the development and application of social theories their surrogate activity. Consequently the theories are designed to serve the needs of the theorists more than the needs of any people who may be unlucky enough to live in a society on which the theories are imposed.

98. One more point to be made in this section: It should not be assumed that a person has enough freedom just because he SAYS he has enough. Freedom is restricted in part by psychological controls of which people are unconscious, and moreover many people's ideas of what constitutes freedom are governed more by social convention than by their real needs. For example, it's likely that many leftists of the oversocialized type would say that most people, including themselves, are socialized too little rather than too much, yet the oversocialized leftist pays a heavy psychological price for his high level of socialization.

SOME PRINCIPLES OF HISTORY

99. Think of history as being the sum of two components: an erratic component that consists of unpredictable events that follow no discernible pattern, and a regular component that consists of long-term historical trends. Here we are concerned with the long-term trends.

100. FIRST PRINCIPLE. If a SMALL change is made that affects a long-term historical trend, then the effect of that change will almost always be transitory—the trend will soon revert to its original state. (Example: A reform movement designed to clean up political corruption in a society rarely has more than a short-term effect; sooner or later the reformers relax and corruption creeps back in. The level of political corruption in a given society tends to remain constant, or to change only slowly with the evolution of the society. Normally, a political cleanup will be permanent only if accompanied by widespread social changes; a SMALL change in the society won't be enough.) If a small change in a long-term historical trend appears to be permanent, it is only because the change acts in the direction in which the trend is already moving, so that the trend is not altered by only pushed a step ahead.

101. The first principle is almost a tautology. If a trend were not stable with respect to small changes, it would wander at random rather than following a definite direction; in other words it would not be a long- term trend at all.

102. SECOND PRINCIPLE. If a change is made that is sufficiently large to alter permanently a long-term historical trend, then it will alter the society as a whole. In other words, a society is a system in which all parts are interrelated, and you can't permanently change any important part without changing all other parts as well.

103. THIRD PRINCIPLE. If a change is made that is large enough to alter permanently a long-term trend, then the consequences for the society as a whole cannot be predicted in advance. (Unless various other societies have passed through the same change and have all experienced the same consequences, in which case one can predict on empirical grounds that another society that passes through the same change will be like to experience similar consequences.)

104. FOURTH PRINCIPLE. A new kind of society cannot be designed on paper. That is, you cannot plan out a new form of society in advance, then set it up and expect it to function as it was designed to do.

105. The third and fourth principles result from the complexity of human societies. A change in human behavior will affect the economy of a society and its physical environment; the economy will affect the environment and vice versa, and the changes in the economy and the environment will affect human behavior in complex, unpredictable ways; and so forth. The network of causes and effects is far too complex to be untangled and understood.

106. FIFTH PRINCIPLE. People do not consciously and rationally choose the form of their society. Societies develop through processes of social evolution that are not under rational human control.

107. The fifth principle is a consequence of the other four.

108. To illustrate: By the first principle, generally speaking an attempt at social reform either acts in the direction in which the society is developing anyway (so that it merely accelerates a change that would have occurred in any case) or else it has only a transitory effect, so that the society soon slips back into its old groove. To make a lasting change in the direction of development of any important aspect of a society, reform is insufficient and revolution is required. (A revolution does not necessarily involve an armed uprising or the overthrow of a government.) By the second principle, a revolution never changes only one aspect of a society, it changes the whole society; and by the third principle changes occur that were never expected or desired by the revolutionaries. By the fourth principle, when revolutionaries or utopians set up a new kind of society, it never works out as planned.

109. The American Revolution does not provide a counterexample. The American "Revolution" was not a revolution in our sense of the word, but a war of independence followed by a rather far-reaching political reform. The Founding Fathers did not change the direction of development of American society, nor did they aspire to do so. They only freed the development of American society from the retarding effect of British rule. Their political reform did not change any basic trend, but only pushed American political culture along its natural direction of development. British society, of which American society was an offshoot, had been moving for a long time in the direction of representative democracy. And prior to the War of Independence the Americans were already practicing a significant degree of representative democracy in the colonial assemblies. The political system established by the Constitution was modeled on the British system and on the colonial assemblies. With major alteration, to be sure—there is no doubt that the Founding Fathers took a very important step. But it was a step along the road that English-speaking world was already traveling. The proof is that Britain and all of its colonies that were populated predominantly by people of British descent ended up with systems of representative democracy essentially similar to that of the United States. If the Founding Fathers had lost their nerve and declined to sign the Declaration of

Independence, our way of life today would not have been significantly different. Maybe we would have had somewhat closer ties to Britain, and would have had a Parliament and Prime Minister instead of a Congress and President. No big deal. Thus the American Revolution provides not a counterexample to our principles but a good illustration of them.

110. Still, one has to use common sense in applying the principles. They are expressed in imprecise language that allows latitude for interpretation, and exceptions to them can be found. So we present these principles not as inviolable laws but as rules of thumb, or guides to thinking, that may provide a partial antidote to naive ideas about the future of society. The principles should be borne constantly in mind, and whenever one reaches a conclusion that conflicts with them one should carefully reexamine one's thinking and retain the conclusion only if one has good, solid reasons for doing so.

INDUSTRIAL-TECHNOLOGICAL SOCIETY CANNOT BE REFORMED

111. The foregoing principles help to show how hopelessly difficult it would be to reform the industrial system in such a way as to prevent it from progressively narrowing our sphere of freedom. There has been a consistent tendency, going back at least to the Industrial Revolution for technology to strengthen the system at a high cost in individual freedom and local autonomy. Hence any change designed to protect freedom from technology would be contrary to a fundamental trend in the development of our society. Consequently, such a change either would be a transitory one—soon swamped by the tide of history—or, if large enough to be permanent would alter the nature of our whole society. This by the first and second principles. Moreover, since society would be altered in a way that could not be predicted in advance (third principle) there would be great risk. Changes large enough to make a lasting difference in favor of freedom would not be initiated because it would be realized that they would gravely disrupt the system. So any attempts at reform would be too timid to be effective. Even if changes large enough to make a lasting difference were initiated, they would be retracted when their disruptive effects became apparent. Thus, permanent changes in favor of freedom could be brought about only by persons prepared to accept radical, dangerous and unpredictable alteration of the entire system. In other words by revolutionaries, not reformers.

112. People anxious to rescue freedom without sacrificing the supposed benefits of technology will suggest naive schemes for some new form of society that would reconcile freedom with technology. Apart from the fact that people who make such suggestions seldom propose any practical means by which the new form of society could be set up in the first place, it follows from the fourth principle that even if the new form of society could be once established, it either would collapse or would give results very different from those expected.

113. So even on very general grounds it seems highly improbable that any way of changing society could be found that would reconcile freedom with modern technology. In the next few sections we will give more specific reasons for concluding that freedom and technological progress are incompatible.

RESTRICTION OF FREEDOM IS
UNAVOIDABLE IN INDUSTRIAL SOCIETY

114. As explained in paragraphs 65-67, 70-73, modern man is strapped down by a network of rules and regulations, and his fate depends on the actions of persons remote from him whose decisions he cannot influence. This is not accidental or a result of the arbitrariness of arrogant bureaucrats. It is necessary and inevitable in any technologically advanced society. The system HAS TO regulate human behavior closely in order to function. At work people have to do what they are told to do, otherwise production would be thrown into chaos. Bureaucracies HAVE TO be run according to rigid rules. To allow any substantial personal discretion to lower-level bureaucrats would disrupt the system and lead to charges of unfairness due to differences in the way individual bureaucrats exercised their discretion. It is true that some restrictions on our freedom could be eliminated, but GENERALLY SPEAKING the regulation of our lives by large organizations is necessary for the functioning of industrial-technological society. The result is a sense of powerlessness on the part of the average person. It may be, however, that formal regulations will tend increasingly to be replaced by psychological tools that make us want to do what the system requires of us. (Propaganda [14], educational techniques, "mental health" programs, etc.)

115. The system HAS TO force people to behave in ways that are increasingly remote from the natural pattern of human behavior. For example, the system needs scientists, mathematicians and engineers. It can't function without them. So heavy pressure is put on children to excel in these fields. It isn't natural for an adolescent human being to spend the bulk of his time sitting at a desk absorbed in study. A normal adolescent wants to spend his time in active contact with the real world. Among primitive peoples the things that children are trained to do tend to be in reasonable harmony with natural human impulses. Among the American Indians, for example, boys were trained in active outdoor pursuits—

just the sort of thing that boys like. But in our society children are pushed into studying technical subjects, which most do grudgingly.

116. Because of the constant pressure that the system exerts to modify human behavior, there is a gradual increase in the number of people who cannot or will not adjust to society's requirements: welfare leeches, youth-gang members, cultists, anti-government rebels, radical environmentalist saboteurs, dropouts and resisters of various kinds.

117. In any technologically advanced society the individual's fate MUST depend on decisions that he personally cannot influence to any great extent. A technological society cannot be broken down into small, autonomous communities, because production depends on the cooperation of very large numbers of people and machines. Such a society MUST be highly organized and decisions HAVE TO be made that affect very large numbers of people. When a decision affects, say, a million people, then each of the affected individuals has, on the average, only a one-millionth share in making the decision. What usually happens in practice is that decisions are made by public officials or corporation executives, or by technical specialists, but even when the public votes on a decision the number of voters ordinarily is too large for the vote of any one individual to be significant. [17] Thus most individuals are unable to influence measurably the major decisions that affect their lives. There is no conceivable way to remedy this in a technologically advanced society. The system tries to "solve" this problem by using propaganda to make people WANT the decisions that have been made for them, but even if this "solution" were completely successful in making people feel better, it would be demeaning.

118. Conservatives and some others advocate more "local autonomy." Local communities once did have autonomy, but such autonomy becomes less and less possible as local communities become more enmeshed with and dependent on large-scale systems like public utilities, computer networks, highway systems, the mass communications media, the modern health care system. Also operating against autonomy is the fact that technology applied in one location often affects people at other locations far way. Thus pesticide or chemical use near a creek may contaminate the water supply hundreds of miles downstream, and the greenhouse effect affects the whole world.

119. The system does not and cannot exist to satisfy human needs. Instead, it is human behavior that has to be modified to fit the needs of the system. This has nothing to do with the political or social ideology that may pretend to guide the technological system. It is the fault of technology, because the system is guided not by ideology but by technical necessity. [18] Of course the system does satisfy many human needs, but generally speaking it does this only to the extend that it is to the advantage of the system to do it. It is the needs of the system that are paramount, not those of the human being. For example, the system provides people with food because the system couldn't function if everyone starved; it attends to people's psychological needs whenever it can CONVENIENTLY do so, because it couldn't function if too many people became depressed or rebellious. But the system, for good, solid, practical reasons, must exert constant pressure on people to mold their behavior to the needs of the system. To much waste accumulating? The government, the media, the educational system, environmentalists, everyone inundates us with a mass of propaganda about recycling. Need more technical personnel? A chorus of voices exhorts kids to study science. No one stops to ask whether it is inhumane to force adolescents to spend the bulk of their time studying subjects most of them hate. When skilled workers are put out of a job by technical advances and have to undergo "retraining," no one asks whether it is humiliating for them to be pushed around in this way. It is simply taken for granted that everyone must bow to technical necessity. and for good reason: If human needs were put before technical necessity there would be economic problems, unemployment, shortages or worse. The concept of "mental health" in our society is

defined largely by the extent to which an individual behaves in accord with the needs of the system and does so without showing signs of stress.

120. Efforts to make room for a sense of purpose and for autonomy within the system are no better than a joke. For example, one company, instead of having each of its employees assemble only one section of a catalogue, had each assemble a whole catalogue, and this was supposed to give them a sense of purpose and achievement. Some companies have tried to give their employees more autonomy in their work, but for practical reasons this usually can be done only to a very limited extent, and in any case employees are never given autonomy as to ultimate goals—their "autonomous" efforts can never be directed toward goals that they select personally, but only toward their employer's goals, such as the survival and growth of the company. Any company would soon go out of business if it permitted its employees to act otherwise. Similarly, in any enterprise within a socialist system, workers must direct their efforts toward the goals of the enterprise, otherwise the enterprise will not serve its purpose as part of the system. Once again, for purely technical reasons it is not possible for most individuals or small groups to have much autonomy in industrial society. Even the small-business owner commonly has only limited autonomy. Apart from the necessity of government regulation, he is restricted by the fact that he must fit into the economic system and conform to its requirements. For instance, when someone develops a new technology, the small-business person often has to use that technology whether he wants to or not, in order to remain competitive.

THE 'BAD' PARTS OF TECHNOLOGY CANNOT BE SEPARATED FROM THE 'GOOD' PARTS

121. A further reason why industrial society cannot be reformed in favor of freedom is that modern technology is a unified system in which all parts are dependent on one another. You can't get rid of the "bad" parts of technology and retain only the "good" parts. Take modern medicine, for example. Progress in medical science depends on progress in chemistry, physics, biology, computer science and other fields. Advanced medical treatments require expensive, high-tech equipment that can be made available only by a technologically progressive, economically rich society. Clearly you can't have much progress in medicine without the whole technological system and everything that goes with it.

122. Even if medical progress could be maintained without the rest of the technological system, it would by itself bring certain evils. Suppose for example that a cure for diabetes is discovered. People with a genetic tendency to diabetes will then be able to survive and reproduce as well as anyone else. Natural selection against genes for diabetes will cease and such genes will spread throughout the population. (This may be occurring to some extent already, since diabetes, while not curable, can be controlled through use of insulin.) The same thing will happen with many other diseases susceptibility to which is affected by genetic degradation of the population. The only solution will be some sort of eugenics program or extensive genetic engineering of human beings, so that man in the future will no longer be a creation of nature, or of chance, or of God (depending on your religious or philosophical opinions), but a manufactured product.

123. If you think that big government interferes in your life too much NOW, just wait till the government starts regulating the genetic constitution of your children. Such regulation will inevitably follow the introduction of genetic engineering of human beings, because the consequences of unregulated genetic engineering would be disastrous. [19]

124. The usual response to such concerns is to talk about "medical ethics." But a code of ethics would not serve to protect freedom in the face of medical progress; it would only make matters worse. A code of ethics applicable to genetic engineering would be in effect a means of regulating the genetic constitution of human beings. Somebody (probably the upper-middle class, mostly) would decide that such and such applications of genetic engineering were "ethical" and others were not, so that in effect they would be imposing their own values on the genetic constitution of the population at large. Even if a code of ethics were chosen on a completely democratic basis, the majority would be imposing their own values on any minorities who might have a different idea of what constituted an "ethical" use of genetic engineering.

The only code of ethics that would truly protect freedom would be one that prohibited ANY genetic engineering of human beings, and you can be sure that no such code will ever be applied in a technological society. No code that reduced genetic engineering to a minor role could stand up for long, because the temptation presented by the immense power of biotechnology would be irresistible, especially since to the majority of people many of its applications will seem obviously and unequivocally good (eliminating physical and mental diseases, giving people the abilities they need to get along in today's world). Inevitably, genetic engineering will be used extensively, but only in ways consistent with the needs of the industrial-technological system. [20]

TECHNOLOGY IS A MORE POWERFUL SOCIAL FORCE THAN THE ASPIRATION FOR FREEDOM

125. It is not possible to make a LASTING compromise between technology and freedom, because technology is by far the more powerful social force and continually encroaches on freedom through REPEATED compromises. Imagine the case of two neighbors, each of whom at the outset owns the same amount of land, but one of whom is more powerful than the other. The powerful one demands a piece of the other's land. The weak one refuses. The powerful one says, "OK, let's compromise. Give me half of what I asked." The weak one has little choice but to give in. Some time later the powerful neighbor demands another piece of land, again there is a compromise, and so forth. By forcing a long series of compromises on the weaker man, the powerful one eventually gets all of his land. So it goes in the conflict between technology and freedom.

126. Let us explain why technology is a more powerful social force than the aspiration for freedom.

127. A technological advance that appears not to threaten freedom often turns out to threaten it very seriously later on. For example, consider motorized transport. A walking man formerly could go where he pleased, go at his own pace without observing any traffic regulations, and was independent of technological support-systems. When motor vehicles were introduced they appeared to increase man's freedom. They took no freedom away from the walking man, no one had to have an automobile if he didn't want one, and anyone who did choose to buy an automobile could travel much faster and farther than a walking man. But the introduction of motorized transport soon changed society in such a way as to restrict greatly man's freedom of locomotion. When automobiles became numerous, it became necessary to regulate their use extensively. In a car, especially in densely populated areas, one cannot just go where one likes at one's own pace one's movement is governed by the flow of traffic and by various traffic laws. One is tied down by various obligations: license requirements, driver test, renewing registration, insurance, maintenance required for safety, monthly payments on purchase price. Moreover, the use of motorized transport is no longer optional Since the introduction of motorized transport the arrangement of our cities has changed in such a way that the majority of people no longer live within walking distance of their place of employment, shopping areas and recreational opportunities, so that they HAVE TO depend on the automobile for transportation. Or else they must use public transportation, in which case they have even less control over their own movement than when driving a car. Even the walker's freedom is now greatly restricted. In the city he continually has to stop to wait for traffic lights that are designed mainly to serve auto traffic. In the country, motor traffic makes it dangerous and unpleasant to walk along the highway. (Note this important point that we have just illustrated with the case of motorized transport: When a new item of

technology is introduced as an option that an individual can accept or not as he chooses, it does not necessarily REMAIN optional. In many cases the new technology changes society in such a way that people eventually find themselves FORCED to use it.)

128. While technological progress AS A WHOLE continually narrows our sphere of freedom, each new technical advance CONSIDERED BY ITSELF appears to be desirable. Electricity, indoor plumbing, rapid long-distance communications ... how could one argue against any of these things, or against any other of the innumerable technical advances that have made modern society? It would have been absurd to resist the introduction of the telephone, for example. It offered many advantages and no disadvantages. Yet, as we explained in paragraphs 59-76, all these technical advances taken together have created a world in which the average man's fate is no longer in his own hands or in the hands of his neighbors and friends, but in those of politicians, corporation executives and remote, anonymous technicians and bureaucrats whom he as an individual has no power to influence. [21] The same process will continue in the future. Take genetic engineering, for example. Few people will resist the introduction of a genetic technique that eliminates a hereditary disease. It does no apparent harm and prevents much suffering. Yet a large number of genetic improvements taken together will make the human being into an engineered product rather than a free creation of chance (or of God, or whatever, depending on your religious beliefs).

129. Another reason why technology is such a powerful social force is that, within the context of a given society, technological progress marches in only one direction; it can never be reversed. Once a technical innovation has been introduced, people usually become dependent on it, so that they can never again do without it, unless it is replaced by some still more advanced innovation. Not only do people become dependent as individuals on a new item of technology, but, even more, the system as a whole becomes dependent on it. (Imagine what would happen to the system today if computers, for example, were eliminated.) Thus the system can move in only one direction, toward greater technologization. Technology repeatedly forces freedom to take a step back, but technology can never take a step back—short of the overthrow of the whole technological system.

130. Technology advances with great rapidity and threatens freedom at many different points at the same time (crowding, rules and regulations, increasing dependence of individuals on large organizations, propaganda and other psychological techniques, genetic engineering, invasion of privacy through surveillance devices and computers, etc.). To hold back any ONE of the threats to freedom would require a long and difficult social struggle. Those who want to protect freedom are overwhelmed by the sheer number of new attacks and the rapidity with which they develop, hence they become apathetic and no longer resist. To fight each of the threats separately would be futile. Success can be hoped for only by fighting the technological system as a whole; but that is revolution, not reform.

131. Technicians (we use this term in its broad sense to describe all those who perform a specialized task that requires training) tend to be so involved in their work (their surrogate activity) that when a conflict arises between their technical work and freedom, they almost always decide in favor of their technical work. This is obvious in the case of scientists, but it also appears elsewhere: Educators, humanitarian groups, conservation organizations do not hesitate to use propaganda or other psychological techniques to help them achieve their laudable ends. Corporations and government agencies, when they find it useful, do not hesitate to collect information about individuals without regard to their privacy. Law enforcement agencies are frequently inconvenienced by the constitutional rights of suspects and often of completely innocent persons, and they do whatever they can do legally (or sometimes illegally) to restrict or circumvent those rights. Most of these educators, government officials and law officers believe in freedom, privacy and constitutional rights, but when these conflict with their work, they usually feel that their work is more important.

132. It is well known that people generally work better and more persistently when striving for a reward than when attempting to avoid a punishment or negative outcome. Scientists and other technicians are motivated mainly by the rewards they get through their work. But those who oppose technological invasions of freedom are working to avoid a negative outcome, consequently there are few who work persistently and well at this discouraging task. If reformers ever achieved a signal victory that seemed to set up a solid barrier against further erosion of freedom through technical progress, most would tend to relax and turn their attention to more agreeable pursuits. But the scientists would remain busy in their laboratories, and technology as it progresses would find ways, in spite of any barriers, to exert more and more control over individuals and make them always more dependent on the system.

133. No social arrangements, whether laws, institutions, customs or ethical codes, can provide permanent protection against technology. History shows that all social arrangements are transitory; they all change or break down eventually. But technological advances are permanent within the context of a given civilization. Suppose for example that it were possible to arrive at some social arrangements that would prevent genetic engineering from being applied to human beings, or prevent it from being applied in such a way as to threaten freedom and dignity. Still, the technology would remain waiting. Sooner or later the social arrangement would break down. Probably sooner, given the pace of change in our society. Then genetic engineering would begin to invade our sphere of freedom, and this invasion would be irreversible (short of a breakdown of technological civilization itself). Any illusions about achieving anything permanent through social arrangements should be dispelled by what is currently happening with environmental legislation. A few years ago its seemed that there were secure legal barriers preventing at least SOME of the worst forms of environmental degradation. A change in the political wind, and those barriers begin to crumble.

134. For all of the foregoing reasons, technology is a more powerful social force than the aspiration for freedom. But this statement requires an important qualification. It appears that during the next several decades the industrial-technological system will be undergoing severe stresses due to economic and environmental problems, and especially due to problems of human behavior (alienation, rebellion, hostility, a variety of social and psychological difficulties). We hope that the stresses through which the system is likely to pass will cause it to break down, or at least will weaken it sufficiently so that a revolution against it becomes possible. If such a revolution occurs and is successful, then at that particular moment the aspiration for freedom will have proved more powerful than technology.

135. In paragraph 125 we used an analogy of a weak neighbor who is left destitute by a strong neighbor who takes all his land by forcing on him a series of compromises. But suppose now that the strong neighbor gets sick, so that he is unable to defend himself. The weak neighbor can force the strong one to give him his land back, or he can kill him. If he lets the strong man survive and only forces him to give the land back, he is a fool, because when the strong man gets well he will again take all the land for himself. The only sensible alternative for the weaker man is to kill the strong one while he has the chance. In the same way, while the industrial system is sick we must destroy it. If we compromise with it and let it recover from its sickness, it will eventually wipe out all of our freedom.

SIMPLER SOCIAL PROBLEMS
HAVE PROVED INTRACTABLE

136. If anyone still imagines that it would be possible to reform the system in such a way as to protect freedom from technology, let him consider how clumsily and for the most part unsuccessfully our society has dealt with other social problems that are far more simple and straightforward. Among other things, the system has failed to stop environmental degradation, political corruption, drug trafficking or domestic abuse.

137. Take our environmental problems, for example. Here the conflict of values is straightforward: economic expedience now versus saving some of our natural resources for our grandchildren. [22] But on this subject we get only a lot of blather and obfuscation from the people who have power, and nothing like a clear, consistent line of action, and we keep on piling up environmental problems that our grandchildren will have to live with. Attempts to resolve the environmental issue consist of struggles and compromises between different factions, some of which are ascendant at one moment, others at another moment. The line of struggle changes with the shifting currents of public opinion. This is not a rational process, nor is it one that is likely to lead to a timely and successful solution to the problem. Major social problems, if they get "solved" at all, are rarely or never solved through any rational, comprehensive plan. They just work themselves out through a process in which various competing groups pursuing their own (usually short- term) self-interest [23] arrive (mainly by luck) at some more or less stable modus vivendi. In fact, the principles we formulated in paragraphs 100-106 make it seem doubtful that rational, long-term social planning can EVER be successful.

138. Thus it is clear that the human race has at best a very limited capacity for solving even relatively straightforward social problems. How then is it going to solve the far more difficult and subtle problem of reconciling freedom with technology? Technology presents clear-cut material advantages, whereas freedom is an abstraction that means different things to different people, and its loss is easily obscured by propaganda and fancy talk.

139. And note this important difference: It is conceivable that our environmental problems (for example) may some day be settled through a rational, comprehensive plan, but if this happens it will be only because it is in the long-term interest of the system to solve these problems. But it is NOT in the interest of the system to preserve freedom or small-group autonomy. On the contrary, it is in the interest of the system to bring human behavior under control to the greatest possible extent. [24] Thus, while practical considerations may eventually force the system to take a rational, prudent approach to environmental problems, equally practical

considerations will force the system to regulate human behavior ever more closely (preferably by indirect means that will disguise the encroachment on freedom). This isn't just our opinion. Eminent social scientists (e.g. James Q. Wilson) have stressed the importance of "socializing" people more effectively.

REVOLUTION IS EASIER THAN REFORM

140. We hope we have convinced the reader that the system cannot be reformed in such a way as to reconcile freedom with technology. The only way out is to dispense with the industrial-technological system altogether. This implies revolution, not necessarily an armed uprising, but certainly a radical and fundamental change in the nature of society.

141. People tend to assume that because a revolution involves a much greater change than reform does, it is more difficult to bring about than reform is. Actually, under certain circumstances revolution is much easier than reform. The reason is that a revolutionary movement can inspire an intensity of commitment that a reform movement cannot inspire. A reform movement merely offers to solve a particular social problem. A revolutionary movement offers to solve all problems at one stroke and create a whole new world; it provides the kind of ideal for which people will take great risks and make great sacrifices. For this reasons it would be much easier to overthrow the whole technological system than to put effective, permanent restraints on the development or application of any one segment of technology, such as genetic engineering, for example. Not many people will devote themselves with single-minded passion to imposing and maintaining restraints on genetic engineering, but under suitable conditions large numbers of people may devote themselves passionately to a revolution against the industrial-technological system. As we noted in paragraph 132, reformers seeking to limit certain aspects of technology would be working to avoid a negative outcome. But revolutionaries work to gain a powerful reward—fulfillment of their revolutionary vision—and therefore work harder and more persistently than reformers do.

142. Reform is always restrained by the fear of painful consequences if changes go too far. But once a revolutionary fever has taken hold of a society, people are willing to undergo unlimited hardships for the sake of their revolution. This was clearly shown in the French and Russian Revolutions. It may be that in such cases only a minority of the population is really committed to the revolution, but this minority is sufficiently large and active so that it becomes the dominant force in society. We will have more to say about revolution in paragraphs 180-205.

CONTROL OF HUMAN BEHAVIOR

143. Since the beginning of civilization, organized societies have had to put pressures on human beings of the sake of the functioning of the social organism. The kinds of pressures vary greatly from one society to another. Some of the pressures are physical (poor diet, excessive labor, environmental pollution), some are psychological (noise, crowding, forcing human behavior into the mold that society requires). In the past, human nature has been approximately constant, or at any rate has varied only within certain bounds. Consequently, societies have been able to push people only up to certain limits. When the limit of human endurance has been passed, things start going wrong: rebellion, or crime, or corruption, or evasion of work, or depression and other mental problems, or an elevated death rate, or a declining birth rate or something else, so that either the society breaks down, or its functioning becomes too inefficient and it is (quickly or gradually, through conquest, attrition or evolution) replaced by some more efficient form of society. [25]

144. Thus human nature has in the past put certain limits on the development of societies. People could be pushed only so far and no farther. But today this may be changing, because modern technology is developing ways of modifying human beings.

145. Imagine a society that subjects people to conditions that make them terribly unhappy, then gives them drugs to take away their unhappiness. Science fiction? It is already happening to some extent in our own society. It is well known that the rate of clinical depression has been greatly increasing in recent decades. We believe that this is due to disruption of the power process, as explained in paragraphs 59-76. But even if we are wrong, the increasing rate of depression is certainly the result of SOME conditions that exist in today's society. Instead of removing the conditions that make people depressed, modern society gives them antidepressant drugs. In effect, antidepressants are a means of modifying an individual's internal state in such a way as to enable him to tolerate social conditions that he would otherwise find intolerable. (Yes, we know that depression is often of purely genetic origin. We are referring here to those cases in which environment plays the predominant role.)

146. Drugs that affect the mind are only one example of the new methods of controlling human behavior that modern society is developing. Let us look at some of the other methods.

147. To start with, there are the techniques of surveillance. Hidden video cameras are now used in most stores and in many other places, computers are used to collect and process vast amounts of information about individuals.

Information so obtained greatly increases the effectiveness of physical coercion (i.e., law enforcement). [26] Then there are the methods of propaganda, for which the mass communication media provide effective vehicles. Efficient techniques have been developed for winning elections, selling products, influencing public opinion. The entertainment industry serves as an important psychological tool of the system, possibly even when it is dishing out large amounts of sex and violence. Entertainment provides modern man with an essential means of escape. While absorbed in television, videos, etc., he can forget stress, anxiety, frustration, dissatisfaction. Many primitive peoples, when they don't have work to do, are quite content to sit for hours at a time doing nothing at all, because they are at peace with themselves and their world. But most modern people must be constantly occupied or entertained, otherwise they get "bored," i.e., they get fidgety, uneasy, irritable.

148. Other techniques strike deeper than the foregoing. Education is no longer a simple affair of paddling a kid's behind when he doesn't know his lessons and patting him on the head when he does know them. It is becoming a scientific technique for controlling the child's development. Sylvan Learning Centers, for example, have had great success in motivating children to study, and psychological techniques are also used with more or less success in many conventional schools. "Parenting" techniques that are taught to parents are designed to make children accept fundamental values of the system and behave in ways that the system finds desirable. "Mental health" programs, "intervention" techniques, psychotherapy and so forth are ostensibly designed to benefit individuals, but in practice they usually serve as methods for inducing individuals to think and behave as the system requires. (There is no contradiction here; an individual whose attitudes or behavior bring him into conflict with the system is up against a force that is too powerful for him to conquer or escape from, hence he is likely to suffer from stress, frustration, defeat. His path will be much easier if he thinks and behaves as the system requires. In that sense the system is acting for the benefit of the individual when it brainwashes him into conformity.) Child abuse in its gross and obvious forms is disapproved in most if not all cultures. Tormenting a child for a trivial reason or no reason at all is something that appalls almost everyone. But many psychologists interpret the concept of abuse much more broadly. Is spanking, when used as part of a rational and consistent system of discipline, a form of abuse? The question will ultimately be decided by whether or not spanking tends to produce behavior that makes a person fit in well with the existing system of society. In practice, the word "abuse" tends to be interpreted to include any method of child-rearing that produces behavior inconvenient for the system. Thus, when they go beyond the prevention of obvious, senseless cruelty, programs for preventing "child abuse" are directed toward the control of human behavior on behalf of the system.

149. Presumably, research will continue to increase the effectiveness of psychological techniques for controlling human behavior. But we think it is unlikely that psychological techniques alone will be sufficient to adjust human beings to the kind of society that technology is creating. Biological

methods probably will have to be used. We have already mentioned the use of drugs in this connection. Neurology may provide other avenues for modifying the human mind. Genetic engineering of human beings is already beginning to occur in the form of "gene therapy," and there is no reason to assume that such methods will not eventually be used to modify those aspects of the body that affect mental functioning.

150. As we mentioned in paragraph 134, industrial society seems likely to be entering a period of severe stress, due in part to problems of human behavior and in part to economic and environmental problems. And a considerable proportion of the system's economic and environmental problems result from the way human beings behave. Alienation, low self-esteem, depression, hostility, rebellion; children who won't study, youth gangs, illegal drug use, rape, child abuse, other crimes, unsafe sex, teen pregnancy, population growth, political corruption, race hatred, ethnic rivalry, bitter ideological conflict (e.g., pro-choice vs. pro- life), political extremism, terrorism, sabotage, anti-government groups, hate groups. All these threaten the very survival of the system. The system will therefore be FORCED to use every practical means of controlling human behavior.

151. The social disruption that we see today is certainly not the result of mere chance. It can only be a result of the conditions of life that the system imposes on people. (We have argued that the most important of these conditions is disruption of the power process.) If the systems succeeds in imposing sufficient control over human behavior to assure its own survival, a new watershed in human history will have been passed. Whereas formerly the limits of human endurance have imposed limits on the development of societies (as we explained in paragraphs 143, 144), industrial-technological society will be able to pass those limits by modifying human beings, whether by psychological methods or biological methods or both. In the future, social systems will not be adjusted to suit the needs of human beings. Instead, human being will be adjusted to suit the needs of the system. [27]

152. Generally speaking, technological control over human behavior will probably not be introduced with a totalitarian intention or even through a conscious desire to restrict human freedom. [28] Each new step in the assertion of control over the human mind will be taken as a rational response to a problem that faces society, such as curing alcoholism, reducing the crime rate or inducing young people to study science and engineering. In many cases there will be a humanitarian justification. For example, when a psychiatrist prescribes an anti-depressant for a depressed patient, he is clearly doing that individual a favor. It would be inhumane to withhold the drug from someone who needs it. When parents send their children to Sylvan Learning Centers to have them manipulated into becoming enthusiastic about their studies, they do so from concern for their children's welfare. It may be that some of these parents wish that one didn't have to have specialized training to get a job and that their kid didn't have to be brainwashed into becoming a computer nerd. But what can they do? They can't change society,

and their child may be unemployable if he doesn't have certain skills. So they send him to Sylvan.

153. Thus control over human behavior will be introduced not by a calculated decision of the authorities but through a process of social evolution (RAPID evolution, however). The process will be impossible to resist, because each advance, considered by itself, will appear to be beneficial, or at least the evil involved in making the advance will appear to be beneficial, or at least the evil involved in making the advance will seem to be less than that which would result from not making it (see paragraph 127). Propaganda for example is used for many good purposes, such as discouraging child abuse or race hatred. [14] Sex education is obviously useful, yet the effect of sex education (to the extent that it is successful) is to take the shaping of sexual attitudes away from the family and put it into the hands of the state as represented by the public school system.

154. Suppose a biological trait is discovered that increases the likelihood that a child will grow up to be a criminal, and suppose some sort of gene therapy can remove this trait. [29] Of course most parents whose children possess the trait will have them undergo the therapy. It would be inhumane to do otherwise, since the child would probably have a miserable life if he grew up to be a criminal. But many or most primitive societies have a low crime rate in comparison with that of our society, even though they have neither high-tech methods of child-rearing nor harsh systems of punishment. Since there is no reason to suppose that more modern men than primitive men have innate predatory tendencies, the high crime rate of our society must be due to the pressures that modern conditions put on people, to which many cannot or will not adjust. Thus a treatment designed to remove potential criminal tendencies is at least in part a way of re-engineering people so that they suit the requirements of the system.

155. Our society tends to regard as a "sickness" any mode of thought or behavior that is inconvenient for the system, and this is plausible because when an individual doesn't fit into the system it causes pain to the individual as well as problems for the system. Thus the manipulation of an individual to adjust him to the system is seen as a "cure" for a "sickness" and therefore as good.

156. In paragraph 127 we pointed out that if the use of a new item of technology is INITIALLY optional, it does not necessarily REMAIN optional, because the new technology tends to change society in such a way that it becomes difficult or impossible for an individual to function without using that technology. This applies also to the technology of human behavior. In a world in which most children are put through a program to make them enthusiastic about studying, a parent will almost be forced to put his kid through such a program, because if he does not, then the kid will grow up to be, comparatively

speaking, an ignoramus and therefore unemployable. Or suppose a biological treatment is discovered that, without undesirable side-effects, will greatly reduce the psychological stress from which so many people suffer in our society. If large numbers of people choose to undergo the treatment, then the general level of stress in society will be reduced, so that it will be possible for the system to increase the stress-producing pressures. In fact, something like this seems to have happened already with one of our society's most important psychological tools for enabling people to reduce (or at least temporarily escape from) stress, namely, mass entertainment (see paragraph 147). Our use of mass entertainment is "optional": No law requires us to watch television, listen to the radio, read magazines. Yet mass entertainment is a means of escape and stress-reduction on which most of us have become dependent. Everyone complains about the trashiness of television, but almost everyone watches it. A few have kicked the TV habit, but it would be a rare person who could get along today without using ANY form of mass entertainment. (Yet until quite recently in human history most people got along very nicely with no other entertainment than that which each local community created for itself.) Without the entertainment industry the system probably would not have been able to get away with putting as much stress-producing pressure on us as it does.

157. Assuming that industrial society survives, it is likely that technology will eventually acquire something approaching complete control over human behavior. It has been established beyond any rational doubt that human thought and behavior have a largely biological basis. As experimenters have demonstrated, feelings such as hunger, pleasure, anger and fear can be turned on and off by electrical stimulation of appropriate parts of the brain. Memories can be destroyed by damaging parts of the brain or they can be brought to the surface by electrical stimulation. Hallucinations can be induced or moods changed by drugs. There may or may not be an immaterial human soul, but if there is one it clearly is less powerful that the biological mechanisms of human behavior. For if that were not the case then researchers would not be able so easily to manipulate human feelings and behavior with drugs and electrical currents.

158. It presumably would be impractical for all people to have electrodes inserted in their heads so that they could be controlled by the authorities. But the fact that human thoughts and feelings are so open to biological intervention shows that the problem of controlling human behavior is mainly a technical problem; a problem of neurons, hormones and complex molecules; the kind of problem that is accessible to scientific attack. Given the outstanding record of our society in solving technical problems, it is overwhelmingly probable that great advances will be made in the control of human behavior.

159. Will public resistance prevent the introduction of technological control of human behavior? It certainly would if an attempt were made to introduce such control all at once. But since technological control will be introduced through a long

sequence of small advances, there will be no rational and effective public resistance. (See paragraphs 127, 132, 153.)

160. To those who think that all this sounds like science fiction, we point out that yesterday's science fiction is today's fact. The Industrial Revolution has radically altered man's environment and way of life, and it is only to be expected that as technology is increasingly applied to the human body and mind, man himself will be altered as radically as his environment and way of life have been.

HUMAN RACE AT A CROSSROADS

161. But we have gotten ahead of our story. It is one thing to develop in the laboratory a series of psychological or biological techniques for manipulating human behavior and quite another to integrate these techniques into a functioning social system. The latter problem is the more difficult of the two. For example, while the techniques of educational psychology doubtless work quite well in the "lab schools" where they are developed, it is not necessarily easy to apply them effectively throughout our educational system. We all know what many of our schools are like. The teachers are too busy taking knives and guns away from the kids to subject them to the latest techniques for making them into computer nerds. Thus, in spite of all its technical advances relating to human behavior, the system to date has not been impressively successful in controlling human beings. The people whose behavior is fairly well under the control of the system are those of the type that might be called "bourgeois." But there are growing numbers of people who in one way or another are rebels against the system: welfare leaches, youth gangs, cultists, satanists, nazis, radical environmentalists, militiamen, etc.

162. The system is currently engaged in a desperate struggle to overcome certain problems that threaten its survival, among which the problems of human behavior are the most important. If the system succeeds in acquiring sufficient control over human behavior quickly enough, it will probably survive. Otherwise it will break down. We think the issue will most likely be resolved within the next several decades, say 40 to 100 years.

163. Suppose the system survives the crisis of the next several decades. By that time it will have to have solved, or at least brought under control, the principal problems that confront it, in particular that of "socializing" human beings; that is, making people sufficiently docile so that heir behavior no longer threatens the system. That being accomplished, it does not appear that there would be any further obstacle to the development of technology, and it would presumably advance toward its logical conclusion, which is complete control over everything on Earth, including human beings and all other important organisms. The system may become a unitary, monolithic organization, or it may be more or less fragmented and consist of a number of organizations coexisting in a relationship that includes elements of both cooperation and competition, just as today the government, the corporations and other large organizations both cooperate and compete with one another. Human freedom mostly will have vanished, because individuals and small groups will be impotent vis-a-vis large organizations armed with supertechnology and an arsenal of advanced psychological and biological tools for manipulating human beings, besides instruments of surveillance and physical coercion. Only a small number of people will have any real power, and even these probably will have only very limited freedom, because their behavior too will be regulated; just as today our politicians

and corporation executives can retain their positions of power only as long as their behavior remains within certain fairly narrow limits.

164. Don't imagine that the systems will stop developing further techniques for controlling human beings and nature once the crisis of the next few decades is over and increasing control is no longer necessary for the system's survival. On the contrary, once the hard times are over the system will increase its control over people and nature more rapidly, because it will no longer be hampered by difficulties of the kind that it is currently experiencing. Survival is not the principal motive for extending control. As we explained in paragraphs 87-90, technicians and scientists carry on their work largely as a surrogate activity; that is, they satisfy their need for power by solving technical problems. They will continue to do this with unabated enthusiasm, and among the most interesting and challenging problems for them to solve will be those of understanding the human body and mind and intervening in their development. For the "good of humanity," of course.

165. But suppose on the other hand that the stresses of the coming decades prove to be too much for the system. If the system breaks down there may be a period of chaos, a "time of troubles" such as those that history has recorded at various epochs in the past. It is impossible to predict what would emerge from such a time of troubles, but at any rate the human race would be given a new chance. The greatest danger is that industrial society may begin to reconstitute itself within the first few years after the breakdown. Certainly there will be many people (power-hungry types especially) who will be anxious to get the factories running again.

166. Therefore two tasks confront those who hate the servitude to which the industrial system is reducing the human race. First, we must work to heighten the social stresses within the system so as to increase the likelihood that it will break down or be weakened sufficiently so that a revolution against it becomes possible. Second, it is necessary to develop and propagate an ideology that opposes technology and the industrial society if and when the system becomes sufficiently weakened. And such an ideology will help to assure that, if and when industrial society breaks down, its remnants will be smashed beyond repair, so that the system cannot be reconstituted. The factories should be destroyed, technical books burned, etc.

HUMAN SUFFERING

167. The industrial system will not break down purely as a result of revolutionary action. It will not be vulnerable to revolutionary attack unless its own internal problems of development lead it into very serious difficulties. So if the system breaks down it will do so either spontaneously, or through a process that is in part spontaneous but helped along by revolutionaries. If the breakdown is sudden, many people will die, since the world's population has become so overblown that it cannot even feed itself any longer without advanced technology. Even if the breakdown is gradual enough so that reduction of the population can occur more through lowering of the birth rate than through elevation of the death rate, the process of de-industrialization probably will be very chaotic and involve much suffering. It is naive to think it likely that technology can be phased out in a smoothly managed, orderly way, especially since the technophiles will fight stubbornly at every step. Is it therefore cruel to work for the breakdown of the system? Maybe, but maybe not. In the first place, revolutionaries will not be able to break the system down unless it is already in enough trouble so that there would be a good chance of its eventually breaking down by itself anyway; and the bigger the system grows, the more disastrous the consequences of its breakdown will be; so it may be that revolutionaries, by hastening the onset of the breakdown, will be reducing the extent of the disaster.

168. In the second place, one has to balance struggle and death against the loss of freedom and dignity. To many of us, freedom and dignity are more important than a long life or avoidance of physical pain. Besides, we all have to die some time, and it may be better to die fighting for survival, or for a cause, than to live a long but empty and purposeless life.

169. In the third place, it is not at all certain that survival of the system will lead to less suffering than breakdown of the system would. The system has already caused, and is continuing to cause, immense suffering all over the world. Ancient cultures, that for hundreds of years gave people a satisfactory relationship with each other and with their environment, have been shattered by contact with industrial society, and the result has been a whole catalogue of economic, environmental, social and psychological problems. One of the effects of the intrusion of industrial society has been that over much of the world traditional controls on population have been thrown out of balance. Hence the population explosion, with all that that implies. Then there is the psychological suffering that is widespread throughout the supposedly fortunate countries of the West (see paragraphs 44, 45). No one knows what will happen as a result of ozone depletion, the greenhouse effect and other environmental problems that cannot yet be foreseen. And, as nuclear proliferation has shown, new technology cannot be kept out of the hands of dictators and irresponsible Third World nations. Would you like to speculate about what Iraq or North Korea will do with genetic engineering?

170. "Oh!" say the technophiles, "Science is going to fix all that! We will conquer famine, eliminate psychological suffering, make everybody healthy and happy!" Yeah, sure. That's what they said 200 years ago. The Industrial Revolution was supposed to eliminate poverty, make everybody happy, etc. The actual result has been quite different. The technophiles are hopelessly naive (or self-deceiving) in their understanding of social problems. They are unaware of (or choose to ignore) the fact that when large changes, even seemingly beneficial ones, are introduced into a society, they lead to a long sequence of other changes, most of which are impossible to predict (paragraph 103). The result is disruption of the society. So it is very probable that in their attempts to end poverty and disease, engineer docile, happy personalities and so forth, the technophiles will create social systems that are terribly troubled, even more so than the present once. For example, the scientists boast that they will end famine by creating new, genetically engineered food plants. But this will allow the human population to keep expanding indefinitely, and it is well known that crowding leads to increased stress and aggression. This is merely one example of the PREDICTABLE problems that will arise. We emphasize that, as past experience has shown, technical progress will lead to other new problems that CANNOT be predicted in advance (paragraph 103). In fact, ever since the Industrial Revolution, technology has been creating new problems for society far more rapidly than it has been solving old ones. Thus it will take a long and difficult period of trial and error for the technophiles to work the bugs out of their Brave New World (if they every do). In the meantime there will be great suffering. So it is not at all clear that the survival of industrial society would involve less suffering than the breakdown of that society would. Technology has gotten the human race into a fix from which there is not likely to be any easy escape.

THE FUTURE

171. But suppose now that industrial society does survive the next several decades and that the bugs do eventually get worked out of the system, so that it functions smoothly. What kind of system will it be? We will consider several possibilities.

172. First let us postulate that the computer scientists succeed in developing intelligent machines that can do all things better than human beings can do them. In that case presumably all work will be done by vast, highly organized systems of machines and no human effort will be necessary. Either of two cases might occur. The machines might be permitted to make all of their own decisions without human oversight, or else human control over the machines might be retained.

173. If the machines are permitted to make all their own decisions, we can't make any conjectures as to the results, because it is impossible to guess how such machines might behave. We only point out that the fate of the human race would be at the mercy of the machines. It might be argued that the human race would never be foolish enough to hand over all power to the machines. But we are suggesting neither that the human race would voluntarily turn power over to the machines nor that the machines would willfully seize power. What we do suggest is that the human race might easily permit itself to drift into a position of such dependence on the machines that it would have no practical choice but to accept all of the machines' decisions. As society and the problems that face it become more and more complex and as machines become more and more intelligent, people will let machines make more and more of their decisions for them, simply because machine-made decisions will bring better results than man-made ones. Eventually a stage may be reached at which the decisions necessary to keep the system running will be so complex that human beings will be incapable of making them intelligently. At that stage the machines will be in effective control. People won't be able to just turn the machines off, because they will be so dependent on them that turning them off would amount to suicide.

174. On the other hand it is possible that human control over the machines may be retained. In that case the average man may have control over certain private machines of his own, such as his car or his personal computer, but control over large systems of machines will be in the hands of a tiny elite—just as it is today, but with two differences. Due to improved techniques the elite will have greater control over the masses; and because human work will no longer be necessary the masses will be superfluous, a useless burden on the system. If the elite is ruthless they may simply decide to exterminate the mass of humanity. If they are humane they may use propaganda or other psychological or biological techniques to reduce the birth rate until the mass of humanity becomes extinct, leaving the world to the elite. Or, if the

elite consists of soft-hearted liberals, they may decide to play the role of good shepherds to the rest of the human race. They will see to it that everyone's physical needs are satisfied, that all children are raised under psychologically hygienic conditions, that everyone has a wholesome hobby to keep him busy, and that anyone who may become dissatisfied undergoes "treatment" to cure his "problem." Of course, life will be so purposeless that people will have to be biologically or psychologically engineered either to remove their need for the power process or to make them "sublimate" their drive for power into some harmless hobby. These engineered human beings may be happy in such a society, but they most certainly will not be free. They will have been reduced to the status of domestic animals.

175. But suppose now that the computer scientists do not succeed in developing artificial intelligence, so that human work remains necessary. Even so, machines will take care of more and more of the simpler tasks so that there will be an increasing surplus of human workers at the lower levels of ability. (We see this happening already. There are many people who find it difficult or impossible to get work, because for intellectual or psychological reasons they cannot acquire the level of training necessary to make themselves useful in the present system.) On those who are employed, ever-increasing demands will be placed: They will need more and more training, more and more ability, and will have to be ever more reliable, conforming and docile, because they will be more and more like cells of a giant organism. Their tasks will be increasingly specialized, so that their work will be, in a sense, out of touch with the real world, being concentrated on one tiny slice of reality. The system will have to use any means that it can, whether psychological or biological, to engineer people to be docile, to have the abilities that the system requires and to "sublimate" their drive for power into some specialized task. But the statement that the people of such a society will have to be docile may require qualification. The society may find competitiveness useful, provided that ways are found of directing competitiveness into channels that serve the needs of the system. We can imagine a future society in which there is endless competition for positions of prestige and power. But no more than a very few people will ever reach the top, where the only real power is (see end of paragraph 163). Very repellent is a society in which a person can satisfy his need for power only by pushing large numbers of other people out of the way and depriving them of THEIR opportunity for power.

176. One can envision scenarios that incorporate aspects of more than one of the possibilities that we have just discussed. For instance, it may be that machines will take over most of the work that is of real, practical importance, but that human beings will be kept busy by being given relatively unimportant work. It has been suggested, for example, that a great development of the service industries might provide work for human beings. Thus people would spent their time shining each other's shoes, driving each other around in taxicabs, making handicrafts for one another, waiting on each other's tables, etc. This seems to us a thoroughly contemptible way for the human race to end up, and we doubt that many people would find fulfilling lives in such pointless busy-work. They would seek other, dangerous

outlets (drugs, crime, "cults," hate groups) unless they were biologically or psychologically engineered to adapt them to such a way of life.

177. Needless to say, the scenarios outlined above do not exhaust all the possibilities. They only indicate the kinds of outcomes that seem to us most likely. But we can envision no plausible scenarios that are any more palatable than the ones we've just described. It is overwhelmingly probable that if the industrial- technological system survives the next 40 to 100 years, it will by that time have developed certain general characteristics: Individuals (at least those of the "bourgeois" type, who are integrated into the system and make it run, and who therefore have all the power) will be more dependent than ever on large organizations; they will be more "socialized" than ever and their physical and mental qualities to a significant extent (possibly to a very great extent) will be those that are engineered into them rather than being the results of chance (or of God's will, or whatever); and whatever may be left of wild nature will be reduced to remnants preserved for scientific study and kept under the supervision and management of scientists (hence it will no longer be truly wild). In the long run (say a few centuries from now) it is likely that neither the human race nor any other important organisms will exist as we know them today, because once you start modifying organisms through genetic engineering there is no reason to stop at any particular point, so that the modifications will probably continue until man and other organisms have been utterly transformed.

178. Whatever else may be the case, it is certain that technology is creating for human beings a new physical and social environment radically different from the spectrum of environments to which natural selection has adapted the human race physically and psychologically. If man is not adjusted to this new environment by being artificially re-engineered, then he will be adapted to it through a long and painful process of natural selection. The former is far more likely than the latter.

179. It would be better to dump the whole stinking system and take the consequences.

STRATEGY

180. The technophiles are taking us all on an utterly reckless ride into the unknown. Many people understand something of what technological progress is doing to us yet take a passive attitude toward it because they think it is inevitable. But we (FC) don't think it is inevitable. We think it can be stopped, and we will give here some indications of how to go about stopping it.

181. As we stated in paragraph 166, the two main tasks for the present are to promote social stress and instability in industrial society and to develop and propagate an ideology that opposes technology and the industrial system. When the system becomes sufficiently stressed and unstable, a revolution against technology may be possible. The pattern would be similar to that of the French and Russian Revolutions. French society and Russian society, for several decades prior to their respective revolutions, showed increasing signs of stress and weakness. Meanwhile, ideologies were being developed that offered a new world view that was quite different from the old one. In the Russian case, revolutionaries were actively working to undermine the old order. Then, when the old system was put under sufficient additional stress (by financial crisis in France, by military defeat in Russia) it was swept away by revolution. What we propose is something along the same lines.

182. It will be objected that the French and Russian Revolutions were failures. But most revolutions have two goals. One is to destroy an old form of society and the other is to set up the new form of society envisioned by the revolutionaries. The French and Russian revolutionaries failed (fortunately!) to create the new kind of society of which they dreamed, but they were quite successful in destroying the old society. We have no illusions about the feasibility of creating a new, ideal form of society. Our goal is only to destroy the existing form of society.

183. But an ideology, in order to gain enthusiastic support, must have a positive ideal as well as a negative one; it must be FOR something as well as AGAINST something. The positive ideal that we propose is Nature. That is, WILD nature: those aspects of the functioning of the Earth and its living things that are independent of human management and free of human interference and control. And with wild nature we include human nature, by which we mean those aspects of the functioning of the human individual that are not subject to regulation by organized society but are products of chance, or free will, or God (depending on your religious or philosophical opinions).

184. Nature makes a perfect counter-ideal to technology for several reasons. Nature (that which is outside the power of the system) is the opposite of technology (which seeks to expand indefinitely the power of the system). Most people will agree that nature is beautiful; certainly it has tremendous popular appeal. The radical environmentalists ALREADY hold an ideology that exalts nature and opposes technology. [30] It is not necessary for the sake of nature to set up some chimerical utopia or any new kind of social order. Nature takes care of itself: It was a spontaneous creation that existed long before any human society, and for countless centuries many different kinds of human societies coexisted with nature without doing it an excessive amount of damage. Only with the Industrial Revolution did the effect of human society on nature become really devastating. To relieve the pressure on nature it is not necessary to create a special kind of social system, it is only necessary to get rid of industrial society. Granted, this will not solve all problems. Industrial society has already done tremendous damage to nature and it will take a very long time for the scars to heal. Besides, even pre-industrial societies can do significant damage to nature. Nevertheless, getting rid of industrial society will accomplish a great deal. It will relieve the worst of the pressure on nature so that the scars can begin to heal. It will remove the capacity of organized society to keep increasing its control over nature (including human nature). Whatever kind of society may exist after the demise of the industrial system, it is certain that most people will live close to nature, because in the absence of advanced technology there is no other way that people CAN live. To feed themselves they must be peasants or herdsmen or fishermen or hunters, etc. And, generally speaking, local autonomy should tend to increase, because lack of advanced technology and rapid communications will limit the capacity of governments or other large organizations to control local communities.

185. As for the negative consequences of eliminating industrial society—well, you can't eat your cake and have it too. To gain one thing you have to sacrifice another.

186. Most people hate psychological conflict. For this reason they avoid doing any serious thinking about difficult social issues, and they like to have such issues presented to them in simple, black-and-white terms: THIS is all good and THAT is all bad. The revolutionary ideology should therefore be developed on two levels.

187. On the more sophisticated level the ideology should address itself to people who are intelligent, thoughtful and rational. The object should be to create a core of people who will be opposed to the industrial system on a rational, thought-out basis, with full appreciation of the problems and ambiguities involved, and of the price that has to be paid for getting rid of the system. It is particularly important to attract people of this type, as they are capable people and will be instrumental in influencing others. These people should be addressed on as rational a level as possible. Facts should never intentionally be distorted and intemperate language

should be avoided. This does not mean that no appeal can be made to the emotions, but in making such appeal care should be taken to avoid misrepresenting the truth or doing anything else that would destroy the intellectual respectability of the ideology.

188. On a second level, the ideology should be propagated in a simplified form that will enable the unthinking majority to see the conflict of technology vs. nature in unambiguous terms. But even on this second level the ideology should not be expressed in language that is so cheap, intemperate or irrational that it alienates people of the thoughtful and rational type. Cheap, intemperate propaganda sometimes achieves impressive short-term gains, but it will be more advantageous in the long run to keep the loyalty of a small number of intelligently committed people than to arouse the passions of an unthinking, fickle mob who will change their attitude as soon as someone comes along with a better propaganda gimmick. However, propaganda of the rabble-rousing type may be necessary when the system is nearing the point of collapse and there is a final struggle between rival ideologies to determine which will become dominant when the old world-view goes under.

189. Prior to that final struggle, the revolutionaries should not expect to have a majority of people on their side. History is made by active, determined minorities, not by the majority, which seldom has a clear and consistent idea of what it really wants. Until the time comes for the final push toward revolution [31], the task of revolutionaries will be less to win the shallow support of the majority than to build a small core of deeply committed people. As for the majority, it will be enough to make them aware of the existence of the new ideology and remind them of it frequently; though of course it will be desirable to get majority support to the extent that this can be done without weakening the core of seriously committed people.

190. Any kind of social conflict helps to destabilize the system, but one should be careful about what kind of conflict one encourages. The line of conflict should be drawn between the mass of the people and the power-holding elite of industrial society (politicians, scientists, upper-level business executives, government officials, etc.). It should NOT be drawn between the revolutionaries and the mass of the people. For example, it would be bad strategy for the revolutionaries to condemn Americans for their habits of consumption. Instead, the average American should be portrayed as a victim of the advertising and marketing industry, which has suckered him into buying a lot of junk that he doesn't need and that is very poor compensation for his lost freedom. Either approach is consistent with the facts. It is merely a matter of attitude whether you blame the advertising industry for manipulating the public or blame the public for allowing itself to be manipulated. As a matter of strategy one should generally avoid blaming the public.

191. One should think twice before encouraging any other social conflict than that between the power- holding elite (which wields technology) and the general public (over which technology exerts its power). For one thing, other

conflicts tend to distract attention from the important conflicts (between power-elite and ordinary people, between technology and nature); for another thing, other conflicts may actually tend to encourage technologization, because each side in such a conflict wants to use

technological power to gain advantages over its adversary. This is clearly seen in rivalries between nations. It also appears in ethnic conflicts within nations. For example, in America many black leaders are anxious to gain power for African Americans by placing back individuals in the technological power-elite. They want there to be many black government officials, scientists, corporation executives and so forth. In this way they are helping to absorb the African American subculture into the technological system. Generally speaking, one should encourage only those social conflicts that can be fitted into the framework of the conflicts of power-elite vs. ordinary people, technology vs nature.

192. But the way to discourage ethnic conflict is NOT through militant advocacy of minority rights (see paragraphs 21, 29). Instead, the revolutionaries should emphasize that although minorities do suffer more or less disadvantage, this disadvantage is of peripheral significance. Our real enemy is the industrial- technological system, and in the struggle against the system, ethnic distinctions are of no importance.

193. The kind of revolution we have in mind will not necessarily involve an armed uprising against any government. It may or may not involve physical violence, but it will not be a POLITICAL revolution. Its focus will be on technology and economics, not politics. [32]

194. Probably the revolutionaries should even AVOID assuming political power, whether by legal or illegal means, until the industrial system is stressed to the danger point and has proved itself to be a failure in the eyes of most people. Suppose for example that some "green" party should win control of the United States Congress in an election. In order to avoid betraying or watering down their own ideology they would have to take vigorous measures to turn economic growth into economic shrinkage. To the average man the results would appear disastrous: There would be massive unemployment, shortages of commodities, etc. Even if the grosser ill effects could be avoided through superhumanly skillful management, still people would have to begin giving up the luxuries to which they have become addicted. Dissatisfaction would grow, the "green" party would be voted out of office and the revolutionaries would have suffered a severe setback. For this reason the revolutionaries should not try to acquire political power until the system has gotten itself into such a mess

that any hardships will be seen as resulting from the failures of the industrial system itself and not from the policies of the revolutionaries. The revolution against technology will probably have to be a revolution by outsiders, a revolution from below and not from above.

195. The revolution must be international and worldwide. It cannot be carried out on a nation-by-nation basis. Whenever it is suggested that the United States, for example, should cut back on technological progress or economic growth, people get hysterical and start screaming that if we fall behind in technology the Japanese will get ahead of us. Holy robots! The world will fly off its orbit if the Japanese ever sell more cars than we do! (Nationalism is a great promoter of technology.) More reasonably, it is argued that if the relatively democratic nations of the world fall behind in technology while nasty, dictatorial nations like China, Vietnam and North Korea continue to progress, eventually the dictators may come to dominate the world. That is why the industrial system should be attacked in all nations simultaneously, to the extent that this may be possible. True, there is no assurance that the industrial system can be destroyed at approximately the same time all over the world, and it is even conceivable that the attempt to overthrow the system could lead instead to the domination of the system by dictators. That is a risk that has to be taken. And it is worth taking, since the difference between a "democratic" industrial system and one controlled by dictators is small compared with the difference between an industrial system and a non-industrial one. [33] It might even be argued that an industrial system controlled by dictators would be preferable, because dictator-controlled systems usually have proved inefficient, hence they are presumably more likely to break down. Look at Cuba.

196. Revolutionaries might consider favoring measures that tend to bind the world economy into a unified whole. Free trade agreements like NAFTA and GATT are probably harmful to the environment in the short run, but in the long run they may perhaps be advantageous because they foster economic interdependence between nations. It will be easier to destroy the industrial system on a worldwide basis if the world economy is so unified that its breakdown in any one major nation will lead to its breakdown in all industrialized nations.

197. Some people take the line that modern man has too much power, too much control over nature; they argue for a more passive attitude on the part of the human race. At best these people are expressing themselves unclearly, because they fail to distinguish between power for LARGE ORGANIZATIONS and power for INDIVIDUALS and SMALL GROUPS. It is a mistake to argue for powerlessness and passivity, because people NEED power. Modern man as a collective entity—that is, the industrial system—has immense power over nature, and we (FC) regard this as evil. But modern INDIVIDUALS and SMALL GROUPS OF INDIVIDUALS have far less power than primitive man ever did. Generally speaking, the vast power of "modern man" over nature is exercised not by individuals or small groups but by large organizations. To the

extent that the average modern INDIVIDUAL can wield the power of technology, he is permitted to do so only within narrow limits and only under the supervision and control of the system. (You need a license for everything and with the license come rules and regulations.) The individual has only those technological powers with which the system chooses to provide him. His PERSONAL power over nature is slight.

198. Primitive INDIVIDUALS and SMALL GROUPS actually had considerable power over nature; or maybe it would be better to say power WITHIN nature. When primitive man needed food he knew how to find and prepare edible roots, how to track game and take it with homemade weapons. He knew how to protect himself from heat, cold, rain, dangerous animals, etc. But primitive man did relatively little damage to nature because the COLLECTIVE power of primitive society was negligible compared to the COLLECTIVE power of industrial society.

199. Instead of arguing for powerlessness and passivity, one should argue that the power of the INDUSTRIAL SYSTEM should be broken, and that this will greatly INCREASE the power and freedom of INDIVIDUALS and SMALL GROUPS.

200. Until the industrial system has been thoroughly wrecked, the destruction of that system must be the revolutionaries' ONLY goal. Other goals would distract attention and energy from the main goal. More importantly, if the revolutionaries permit themselves to have any other goal than the destruction of technology, they will be tempted to use technology as a tool for reaching that other goal. If they give in to that temptation, they will fall right back into the technological trap, because modern technology is a unified, tightly organized system, so that, in order to retain SOME technology, one finds oneself obliged to retain MOST technology, hence one ends up sacrificing only token amounts of technology.

201. Suppose for example that the revolutionaries took "social justice" as a goal. Human nature being what it is, social justice would not come about spontaneously; it would have to be enforced. In order to enforce it the revolutionaries would have to retain central organization and control. For that they would need rapid long-distance transportation and communication, and therefore all the technology needed to support the transportation and communication systems. To feed and clothe poor people they would have to use agricultural and manufacturing technology. And so forth. So that the attempt to insure social justice would force them to retain most parts of the technological system. Not that we have anything against social justice, but it must not be allowed to interfere with the effort to get rid of the technological system.

202. It would be hopeless for revolutionaries to try to attack the system without using SOME modern technology. If nothing else they must use the communications media to spread their message. But they should use modern technology for only ONE purpose: to attack the technological system.

203. Imagine an alcoholic sitting with a barrel of wine in front of him. Suppose he starts saying to himself, "Wine isn't bad for you if used in moderation. Why, they say small amounts of wine are even good for you! It won't do me any harm if I take just one little drink.... " Well you know what is going to happen. Never forget that the human race with technology is just like an alcoholic with a barrel of wine.

204. Revolutionaries should have as many children as they can. There is strong scientific evidence that social attitudes are to a significant extent inherited. No one suggests that a social attitude is a direct outcome of a person's genetic constitution, but it appears that personality traits are partly inherited and that certain personality traits tend, within the context of our society, to make a person more likely to hold this or that social attitude. Objections to these findings have been raised, but the objections are feeble and seem to be ideologically motivated. In any event, no one denies that children tend on the average to hold social attitudes similar to those of their parents. From our point of view it doesn't matter all that much whether the attitudes are passed on genetically or through childhood training. In either case they ARE passed on.

205. The trouble is that many of the people who are inclined to rebel against the industrial system are also concerned about the population problems, hence they are apt to have few or no children. In this way they may be handing the world over to the sort of people who support or at least accept the industrial system. To insure the strength of the next generation of revolutionaries the present generation should reproduce itself abundantly. In doing so they will be worsening the population problem only slightly. And the important problem is to get rid of the industrial system, because once the industrial system is gone the world's population necessarily will decrease (see paragraph 167); whereas, if the industrial system survives, it will continue developing new techniques of food production that may enable the world's population to keep increasing almost indefinitely.

206. With regard to revolutionary strategy, the only points on which we absolutely insist are that the single overriding goal must be the elimination of modern technology, and that no other goal can be allowed to compete with this one. For the rest, revolutionaries should take an empirical approach. If experience indicates that some of the recommendations made in the foregoing paragraphs are not going to give good results, then those recommendations should be discarded.

TWO KINDS OF TECHNOLOGY

207. An argument likely to be raised against our proposed revolution is that it is bound to fail, because (it is claimed) throughout history technology has always progressed, never regressed, hence technological regression is impossible. But this claim is false.

208. We distinguish between two kinds of technology, which we will call small-scale technology and organization-dependent technology. Small-scale technology is technology that can be used by small-scale communities without outside assistance. Organization-dependent technology is technology that depends on large-scale social organization. We are aware of no significant cases of regression in small-scale technology. But organization-dependent technology DOES regress when the social organization on which it depends breaks down. Example: When the Roman Empire fell apart the Romans' small-scale technology survived because any clever village craftsman could build, for instance, a water wheel, any skilled smith could make steel by Roman methods, and so forth. But the Romans' organization-dependent technology DID regress. Their aqueducts fell into disrepair and were never rebuilt. Their techniques of road construction were lost. The Roman system of urban sanitation was forgotten, so that not until rather recent times did the sanitation of European cities equal that of Ancient Rome.

209. The reason why technology has seemed always to progress is that, until perhaps a century or two before the Industrial Revolution, most technology was small-scale technology. But most of the technology developed since the Industrial Revolution is organization-dependent technology. Take the refrigerator for example. Without factory-made parts or the facilities of a post-industrial machine shop it would be virtually impossible for a handful of local craftsmen to build a refrigerator. If by some miracle they did succeed in building one it would be useless to them without a reliable source of electric power. So they would have to dam a stream and build a generator. Generators require large amounts of copper wire. Imagine trying to make that wire without modern machinery. And where would they get a gas suitable for refrigeration? It would be much easier to build an icehouse or preserve food by drying or picking, as was done before the invention of the refrigerator.

210. So it is clear that if the industrial system were once thoroughly broken down, refrigeration technology would quickly be lost. The same is true of other organization-dependent technology. And once this technology had been lost for a generation or so it would take centuries to rebuild it, just as it took centuries to build it the first time around. Surviving technical books would be few and scattered. An industrial society, if built from scratch without outside help, can only be built in a series of stages: You need tools to make tools to make tools to make tools ... . A long process of economic development and progress in social organization is required.

And, even in the absence of an ideology opposed to technology, there is no reason to believe that anyone would be interested in rebuilding industrial society. The enthusiasm for "progress" is a phenomenon peculiar to the modern form of society, and it seems not to have existed prior to the 17th century or thereabouts.

211. In the late Middle Ages there were four main civilizations that were about equally "advanced": Europe, the Islamic world, India, and the Far East (China, Japan, Korea). Three of those civilizations remained more or less stable, and only Europe became dynamic. No one knows why Europe became dynamic at that time; historians have their theories but these are only speculation. At any rate, it is clear that rapid development toward a technological form of society occurs only under special conditions. So there is no reason to assume that a long-lasting technological regression cannot be brought about.

212. Would society EVENTUALLY develop again toward an industrial-technological form? Maybe, but there is no use in worrying about it, since we can't predict or control events 500 or 1,000 years in the future. Those problems must be dealt with by the people who will live at that time.

THE DANGER OF LEFTISM

213. Because of their need for rebellion and for membership in a movement, leftists or persons of similar psychological type often are unattracted to a rebellious or activist movement whose goals and membership are not initially leftist. The resulting influx of leftish types can easily turn a non-leftist movement into a leftist one, so that leftist goals replace or distort the original goals of the movement.

214. To avoid this, a movement that exalts nature and opposes technology must take a resolutely anti-leftist stance and must avoid all collaboration with leftists. Leftism is in the long run inconsistent with wild nature, with human freedom and with the elimination of modern technology. Leftism is collectivist; it seeks to bind together the entire world (both nature and the human race) into a unified whole. But this implies management of nature and of human life by organized society, and it requires advanced technology. You can't have a united world without rapid transportation and communication, you can't make all people love one another without sophisticated psychological techniques, you can't have a "planned society" without the necessary technological base. Above all, leftism is driven by the need for power, and the leftist seeks power on a collective basis, through identification with a mass movement or an organization. Leftism is unlikely ever to give up technology, because technology is too valuable a source of collective power.

215. The anarchist [34] too seeks power, but he seeks it on an individual or small-group basis; he wants individuals and small groups to be able to control the circumstances of their own lives. He opposes technology because it makes small groups dependent on large organizations.

216. Some leftists may seem to oppose technology, but they will oppose it only so long as they are outsiders and the technological system is controlled by non-leftists. If leftism ever becomes dominant in society, so that the technological system becomes a tool in the hands of leftists, they will enthusiastically use it and promote its growth. In doing this they will be repeating a pattern that leftism has shown again and again in the past. When the Bolsheviks in Russia were outsiders, they vigorously opposed censorship and the secret police, they advocated self-determination for ethnic minorities, and so forth; but as soon as they came into power themselves, they imposed a tighter censorship and created a more ruthless secret police than any that had existed under the tsars, and they oppressed ethnic minorities at least as much as the tsars had done. In the United States, a couple of decades ago when leftists were a minority in our universities, leftist professors were vigorous proponents of academic freedom, but today, in those of our universities where leftists have become

dominant, they have shown themselves ready to take away from everyone else's academic freedom. (This is "political correctness.") The same will happen with leftists and technology: They will use it to oppress everyone else if they ever get it under their own control.

217. In earlier revolutions, leftists of the most power-hungry type, repeatedly, have first cooperated with non-leftist revolutionaries, as well as with leftists of a more libertarian inclination, and later have double- crossed them to seize power for themselves. Robespierre did this in the French Revolution, the Bolsheviks did it in the Russian Revolution, the communists did it in Spain in 1938 and Castro and his followers did it in Cuba. Given the past history of leftism, it would be utterly foolish for non-leftist revolutionaries today to collaborate with leftists.

218. Various thinkers have pointed out that leftism is a kind of religion. Leftism is not a religion in the strict sense because leftist doctrine does not postulate the existence of any supernatural being. But, for the leftist, leftism plays a psychological role much like that which religion plays for some people. The leftist NEEDS to believe in leftism; it plays a vital role in his psychological economy. His beliefs are not easily modified by logic or facts. He has a deep conviction that leftism is morally Right with a capital R, and that he has not only a right but a duty to impose leftist morality on everyone. (However, many of the people we are referring to as "leftists" do not think of themselves as leftists and would not describe their system of beliefs as leftism. We use the term "leftism" because we don't know of any better words to designate the spectrum of related creeds that includes the feminist, gay rights, political correctness, etc., movements, and because these movements have a strong affinity with the old left. See paragraphs 227-230.)

219. Leftism is a totalitarian force. Wherever leftism is in a position of power it tends to invade every private corner and force every thought into a leftist mold. In part this is because of the quasi-religious character of leftism; everything contrary to leftist beliefs represents Sin. More importantly, leftism is a totalitarian force because of the leftists' drive for power. The leftist seeks to satisfy his need for power through identification with a social movement and he tries to go through the power process by helping to pursue and attain the goals of the movement (see paragraph 83). But no matter how far the movement has gone in attaining its goals the leftist is never satisfied, because his activism is a surrogate activity (see paragraph 41). That is, the leftist's real motive is not to attain the ostensible goals of leftism; in reality he is motivated by the sense of power he gets from struggling for and then reaching a social goal. [35] Consequently the leftist is never satisfied with the goals he has already attained; his need for the power process leads him always to pursue some new goal. The leftist wants equal opportunities for minorities. When that is attained he insists on statistical equality of achievement by minorities. And as long as anyone harbors in some corner of his mind a negative attitude toward some minority, the leftist has to re-educated him. And ethnic minorities are not

enough; no one can be allowed to have a negative attitude toward homosexuals, disabled people, fat people, old people, ugly people, and on and on and on. It's not enough that the public should be informed about the hazards of smoking; a warning has to be stamped on every package of cigarettes. Then cigarette advertising has to be restricted if not banned. The activists will never be satisfied until tobacco is outlawed, and after that it will be alcohol, then junk food, etc. Activists have fought gross child abuse, which is reasonable. But now they want to stop all spanking. When they have done that they will want to ban something else they consider unwholesome, then another thing and then another. They will never be satisfied until they have complete control over all child rearing practices. And then they will move on to another cause.

220. Suppose you asked leftists to make a list of ALL the things that were wrong with society, and then suppose you instituted EVERY social change that they demanded. It is safe to say that within a couple of years the majority of leftists would find something new to complain about, some new social "evil" to correct because, once again, the leftist is motivated less by distress at society's ills than by the need to satisfy his drive for power by imposing his solutions on society.

221. Because of the restrictions placed on their thoughts and behavior by their high level of socialization, many leftists of the over-socialized type cannot pursue power in the ways that other people do. For them the drive for power has only one morally acceptable outlet, and that is in the struggle to impose their morality on everyone.

222. Leftists, especially those of the oversocialized type, are True Believers in the sense of Eric Hoffer's book, "The True Believer." But not all True Believers are of the same psychological type as leftists. Presumably a true-believing nazi, for instance, is very different psychologically from a true-believing leftist. Because of their capacity for single-minded devotion to a cause, True Believers are a useful, perhaps a necessary, ingredient of any revolutionary movement. This presents a problem with which we must admit we don't know how to deal. We aren't sure how to harness the energies of the True Believer to a revolution against technology. At present all we can say is that no True Believer will make a safe recruit to the revolution unless his commitment is exclusively to the destruction of technology. If he is committed also to another ideal, he may want to use technology as a tool for pursuing that other ideal (see paragraphs 220, 221).

223. Some readers may say, "This stuff about leftism is a lot of crap. I know John and Jane who are leftish types and they don't have all these totalitarian tendencies." It's quite true that many leftists, possibly even a numerical majority, are decent people who sincerely believe in tolerating others' values (up to a point) and wouldn't want to use high-handed methods to reach their social goals. Our remarks about leftism are not meant to apply to every individual leftist but to describe the

general character of leftism as a movement. And the general character of a movement is not necessarily determined by the numerical proportions of the various kinds of people involved in the movement.

224. The people who rise to positions of power in leftist movements tend to be leftists of the most power-hungry type, because power-hungry people are those who strive hardest to get into positions of power. Once the power-hungry types have captured control of the movement, there are many leftists of a gentler breed who inwardly disapprove of many of the actions of the leaders, but cannot bring themselves to oppose them. They NEED their faith in the movement, and because they cannot give up this faith they go along with the leaders. True, SOME leftists do have the guts to oppose the totalitarian tendencies that emerge, but they generally lose, because the power-hungry types are better organized, are more ruthless and Machiavellian and have taken care to build themselves a strong power base.

225. These phenomena appeared clearly in Russia and other countries that were taken over by leftists. Similarly, before the breakdown of communism in the USSR, leftish types in the West would seldom criticize that country. If prodded they would admit that the USSR did many wrong things, but then they would try to find excuses for the communists and begin talking about the faults of the West. They always opposed Western military resistance to communist aggression. Leftish types all over the world vigorously protested the U.S. military action in Vietnam, but when the USSR invaded Afghanistan they did nothing. Not that they approved of the Soviet actions; but because of their leftist faith, they just couldn't bear to put themselves in opposition to communism. Today, in those of our universities where "political correctness" has become dominant, there are probably many leftish types who privately disapprove of the suppression of academic freedom, but they go along with it anyway.

226. Thus the fact that many individual leftists are personally mild and fairly tolerant people by no means prevents leftism as a whole form having a totalitarian tendency.

227. Our discussion of leftism has a serious weakness. It is still far from clear what we mean by the word "leftist." There doesn't seem to be much we can do about this. Today leftism is fragmented into a whole spectrum of activist movements. Yet not all activist movements are leftist, and some activist movements (e.g., radical environmentalism) seem to include both personalities of the leftist type and personalities of thoroughly un-leftist types who ought to know better than to collaborate with leftists. Varieties of leftists fade out gradually into varieties of non-leftists and we ourselves would often be hard-pressed to decide whether a given individual is or is not a leftist. To the extent that it is defined at all, our conception of leftism is defined by the discussion of it that we have given in this article, and we can only advise the reader to use his own judgment in deciding who is a leftist.

228. But it will be helpful to list some criteria for diagnosing leftism. These criteria cannot be applied in a cut and dried manner. Some individuals may meet some of the criteria without being leftists, some leftists may not meet any of the criteria. Again, you just have to use your judgment.

229. The leftist is oriented toward large-scale collectivism. He emphasizes the duty of the individual to serve society and the duty of society to take care of the individual. He has a negative attitude toward individualism. He often takes a moralistic tone. He tends to be for gun control, for sex education and other psychologically "enlightened" educational methods, for social planning, for affirmative action, for multiculturalism. He tends to identify with victims. He tends to be against competition and against violence, but he often finds excuses for those leftists who do commit violence. He is fond of using the common catch-phrases of the left, like "racism," "sexism," "homophobia," "capitalism," "imperialism," "neocolonialism," "genocide," "social change," "social justice," "social responsibility." Maybe the best diagnostic trait of the leftist is his tendency to sympathize with the following movements: feminism, gay rights, ethnic rights, disability rights, animal rights, political correctness. Anyone who strongly sympathizes with ALL of these movements is almost certainly a leftist. [36]

230. The more dangerous leftists, that is, those who are most power-hungry, are often characterized by arrogance or by a dogmatic approach to ideology. However, the most dangerous leftists of all may be certain oversocialized types who avoid irritating displays of aggressiveness and refrain from advertising their leftism, but work quietly and unobtrusively to promote collectivist values, "enlightened" psychological techniques for socializing children, dependence of the individual on the system, and so forth. These crypto-leftists (as we may call them) approximate certain bourgeois types as far as practical action is concerned, but differ from them in psychology, ideology and motivation. The ordinary bourgeois tries to bring people under control of the system in order to protect his way of life, or he does so simply because his attitudes are conventional. The crypto-leftist tries to bring people under control of the system because he is a True Believer in a collectivistic ideology. The crypto-leftist is differentiated from the average leftist of the oversocialized type by the fact that his rebellious impulse is weaker and he is more securely socialized. He is differentiated from the ordinary well-socialized bourgeois by the fact that there is some deep lack within him that makes it necessary for him to devote himself to a cause and immerse himself in a collectivity. And maybe his (well-sublimated) drive for power is stronger than that of the average bourgeois.

FINAL NOTE

231. Throughout this article we've made imprecise statements and statements that ought to have had all sorts of qualifications and reservations attached to them; and some of our statements may be flatly false. Lack of sufficient information and the need for brevity made it impossible for us to formulate our assertions more precisely or add all the necessary qualifications. And of course in a discussion of this kind one must rely heavily on intuitive judgment, and that can sometimes be wrong. So we don't claim that this article expresses more than a crude approximation to the truth.

232. All the same, we are reasonably confident that the general outlines of the picture we have painted here are roughly correct. Just one possible weak point needs to be mentioned. We have portrayed leftism in its modern form as a phenomenon peculiar to our time and as a symptom of the disruption of the power process. But we might possibly be wrong about this. Oversocialized types who try to satisfy their drive for power by imposing their morality on everyone have certainly been around for a long time. But we THINK that the decisive role played by feelings of inferiority, low self-esteem, powerlessness, identification with victims by people who are not themselves victims, is a peculiarity of modern leftism. Identification with victims by people not themselves victims can be seen to some extent in 19th century leftism and early Christianity but as far as we can make out, symptoms of low self-esteem, etc., were not nearly so evident in these movements, or in any other movements, as they are in modern leftism. But we are not in a position to assert confidently that no such movements have existed prior to modern leftism. This is a significant question to which historians ought to give their attention.

Notes

1. (Paragraph 19) We are asserting that ALL, or even most, bullies and ruthless competitors suffer from feelings of inferiority.

2. (Paragraph 25) During the Victorian period many oversocialized people suffered from serious psychological problems as a result of repressing or trying to repress their sexual feelings. Freud apparently based his theories on people of this type. Today the focus of socialization has shifted from sex to aggression.

3. (Paragraph 27) Not necessarily including specialists in engineering or the "hard" sciences.

4. (Paragraph 28) There are many individuals of the middle and upper classes who resist some of these values, but usually their resistance is more or less covert. Such resistance appears in the mass media only to a very limited extent. The main thrust of propaganda in our society is in favor of the stated values.

The main reason why these values have become, so to speak, the official values of our society is that they are useful to the industrial system. Violence is discouraged because it disrupts the functioning of the system. Racism is discouraged because ethnic conflicts also disrupt the system, and discrimination wastes the talents of minority-group members who could be useful to the system. Poverty must be "cured" because the underclass causes problems for the system and contact with the underclass lowers the morale of the other classes. Women are encouraged to have careers because their talents are useful to the system and, more importantly, because by having regular jobs women become better integrated into the system and tied directly to it rather than to their families. This helps to weaken family solidarity. (The leaders of the system say they want to strengthen the family, but they really mean is that they want the family to serve as an effective tool for socializing children in accord with the needs of the system. We argue in paragraphs 51, 52 that the system cannot afford to let the family or other small-scale social groups be strong or autonomous.)

5. (Paragraph 42) It may be argued that the majority of people don't want to make their own decisions but want leaders to do their thinking for them. There is an element of truth in this. People like to make their own decisions in small matters, but making decisions on difficult, fundamental questions requires facing up to psychological conflict, and most people hate psychological conflict. Hence they tend to lean on others in making difficult decisions. But it does not follow that they like to have decisions imposed upon them without having any opportunity to influence

those decisions. The majority of people are natural followers, not leaders, but they like to have direct personal access to their leaders, they want to be able to influence the leaders and participate to some extent in making even the difficult decisions. At least to that degree they need autonomy.

6. (Paragraph 44) Some of the symptoms listed are similar to those shown by caged animals.

To explain how these symptoms arise from deprivation with respect to the power process:

Common-sense understanding of human nature tells one that lack of goals whose attainment requires effort leads to boredom and that boredom, long continued, often leads eventually to depression. Failure to attain goals leads to frustration and lowering of self-esteem. Frustration leads to anger, anger to aggression, often in the form of spouse or child abuse. It has been shown that long-continued frustration commonly leads to depression and that depression tends to cause guilt, sleep disorders, eating disorders and bad feelings about oneself. Those who are tending toward depression seek pleasure as an antidote; hence insatiable hedonism and excessive sex, with perversions as a means of getting new kicks. Boredom too tends to cause excessive pleasure-seeking since, lacking other goals, people often use pleasure as a goal. See accompanying diagram.

The foregoing is a simplification. Reality is more complex, and of course, deprivation with respect to the power process is not the ONLY cause of the symptoms described.

By the way, when we mention depression we do not necessarily mean depression that is severe enough to be treated by a psychiatrist. Often only mild forms of depression are involved. And when we speak of goals we do not necessarily mean long-term, thought-out goals. For many or most people through much of human history, the goals of a hand-to-mouth existence (merely providing oneself and one's family with food from day to day) have been quite sufficient.

7. (Paragraph 52) A partial exception may be made for a few passive, inward-looking groups, such as the Amish, which have little effect on the wider society. Apart from these, some genuine small-scale communities do exist in America today. For instance, youth gangs and "cults." Everyone regards them as dangerous, and so they are, because the members of these groups are loyal primarily to one another rather than to the system, hence the system cannot control them.

Or take the gypsies. The gypsies commonly get away with theft and fraud because their loyalties are such that they can always get other gypsies to give testimony that "proves" their innocence. Obviously the system would be in serious trouble if too many people belonged to such groups.

Some of the early-20th century Chinese thinkers who were concerned with modernizing China recognized the necessity breaking down small-scale social groups such as the family: "(According to Sun Yat-sen) the Chinese people needed a new surge of patriotism, which would lead to a transfer of loyalty from the family to the state.... (According to Li Huang) traditional attachments, particularly to the family had to be abandoned if nationalism were to develop in China." (Chester C. Tan, "Chinese Political Thought in the Twentieth Century," page 125, page 297.)

8. (Paragraph 56) Yes, we know that 19th century America had its problems, and serious ones, but for the sake of brevity we have to express ourselves in simplified terms.

9. (Paragraph 61) We leave aside the "underclass." We are speaking of the mainstream.

10. (Paragraph 62) Some social scientists, educators, "mental health" professionals and the like are doing their best to push the social drives into group 1 by trying to see to it that everyone has a satisfactory social life.

11. (Paragraphs 63, 82) Is the drive for endless material acquisition really an artificial creation of the advertising and marketing industry? Certainly there is no innate human drive for material acquisition. There have been many cultures in which people have desired little material wealth beyond what was necessary to satisfy their basic physical needs (Australian aborigines, traditional Mexican peasant culture, some African cultures). On the other hand there have also been many pre-industrial cultures in which material acquisition has played an important role. So we can't claim that today's acquisition-oriented culture is exclusively a creation of the advertising and marketing industry. But it is clear that the advertising and marketing industry has had an important part in creating that culture. The big corporations that spend millions on advertising wouldn't be spending that kind of money without solid proof that they were getting it back in increased sales. One member of FC met a sales manager a couple of years ago who was frank enough to tell him, "Our job is to make people buy things they don't want and don't need." He then described how an untrained novice could present people with the facts about a product, and make no sales at all, while a trained and experienced professional salesman would make lots of sales to the same people. This shows that people are manipulated into buying things they don't really want.

12. (Paragraph 64) The problem of purposelessness seems to have become less serious during the last 15 years or so, because people now feel less secure physically and economically than they did earlier, and the need for security provides them with a goal. But purposelessness has been replaced by frustration over the difficulty of attaining security. We emphasize the problem of purposelessness because the liberals and leftists would wish to solve our social problems by having society guarantee everyone's security; but if that could be done it would only bring back the problem of purposelessness. The real issue is not whether society provides well or poorly for people's security; the trouble is that people are dependent on the system for their security rather than having it in their own hands. This, by the way, is part of the reason why some people get worked up about the right to bear arms; possession of a gun puts that aspect of their security in their own hands.

13. (Paragraph 66) Conservatives' efforts to decrease the amount of government regulation are of little benefit to the average man. For one thing, only a fraction of the regulations can be eliminated because most regulations are necessary. For another thing, most of the deregulation affects business rather than the average individual, so that its main effect is to take power from the government and give it to private corporations. What this means for the average man is that government interference in his life is replaced by interference from big corporations, which may be permitted, for example, to dump more chemicals that get into his water supply and give him cancer. The conservatives are just taking the average man for a sucker, exploiting his resentment of Big Government to promote the power of Big Business.

14. (Paragraph 73) When someone approves of the purpose for which propaganda is being used in a given case, he generally calls it "education" or applies to it some similar euphemism. But propaganda is propaganda regardless of the purpose for which it is used.

15. (Paragraph 83) We are not expressing approval or disapproval of the Panama invasion. We only use it to illustrate a point.

16. (Paragraph 95) When the American colonies were under British rule there were fewer and less effective legal guarantees of freedom than there were after the American Constitution went into effect, yet there was more personal freedom in pre-industrial America, both before and after the War of Independence, than there was after the Industrial Revolution took hold in this country. We quote from "Violence in America: Historical and Comparative Perspectives," edited by Hugh Davis Graham and Ted Robert Gurr, Chapter 12 by Roger Lane, pages 476-478:

"The progressive heightening of standards of propriety, and with it the increasing reliance on official law enforcement (in 19th century America) ... were common to the whole society.... [T]he change in social behavior is so long term and so widespread as to suggest a connection with the most fundamental of contemporary social processes; that of industrial urbanization itself...."Massachusetts in 1835 had a population of some 660,940, 81 percent rural, overwhelmingly preindustrial and native born. It's citizens were used to considerable personal freedom. Whether teamsters, farmers or artisans, they were all accustomed to setting their own schedules, and the nature of their work made them physically independent of each other.... Individual problems, sins or even crimes, were not generally cause for wider social concern...."But the impact of the twin movements to the city and to the factory, both just gathering force in 1835, had a progressive effect on personal behavior throughout the 19th century and into the 20th. The factory demanded regularity of behavior, a life governed by obedience to the rhythms of clock and calendar, the demands of foreman and supervisor. In the city or town, the needs of living in closely packed neighborhoods inhibited many actions previously unobjectionable. Both blue- and white-collar employees in larger establishments were mutually dependent on their fellows; as one man's work fit into anther's, so one man's business was no longer his own.

"The results of the new organization of life and work were apparent by 1900, when some 76 percent of the 2,805,346 inhabitants of Massachusetts were classified as urbanites. Much violent or irregular behavior which had been tolerable in a casual, independent society was no longer acceptable in the more formalized, cooperative atmosphere of the later period.... The move to the cities had, in short, produced a more tractable, more socialized, more 'civilized' generation than its predecessors."

17. (Paragraph 117) Apologists for the system are fond of citing cases in which elections have been decided by one or two votes, but such cases are rare.

18. (Paragraph 119) "Today, in technologically advanced lands, men live very similar lives in spite of geographical, religious, and political differences. The daily lives of a Christian bank clerk in Chicago, a Buddhist bank clerk in Tokyo, and a Communist bank clerk in Moscow are far more alike than the life of any one of them is like that of any single man who lived a thousand years ago. These similarities are the result of a common technology...." L. Sprague de Camp, "The Ancient Engineers," Ballantine edition, page 17.

The lives of the three bank clerks are not IDENTICAL. Ideology does have SOME effect. But all technological societies, in order to survive, must evolve along APPROXIMATELY the same trajectory.

19. (Paragraph 123) Just think an irresponsible genetic engineer might create a lot of terrorists.

20. (Paragraph 124) For a further example of undesirable consequences of medical progress, suppose a reliable cure for cancer is discovered. Even if the treatment is too expensive to be available to any but the elite, it will greatly reduce their incentive to stop the escape of carcinogens into the environment.

21. (Paragraph 128) Since many people may find paradoxical the notion that a large number of good things can add up to a bad thing, we illustrate with an analogy. Suppose Mr. A is playing chess with Mr. B. Mr. C, a Grand Master, is looking over Mr. A's shoulder. Mr. A of course wants to win his game, so if Mr. C points out a good move for him to make, he is doing Mr. A a favor. But suppose now that Mr. C tells Mr. A how to make ALL of his moves. In each particular instance he does Mr. A a favor by showing him his best move, but by making ALL of his moves for him he spoils his game, since there is not point in Mr. A's playing the game at all if someone else makes all his moves.

The situation of modern man is analogous to that of Mr. A. The system makes an individual's life easier for him in innumerable ways, but in doing so it deprives him of control over his own fate.

22. (Paragraph 137) Here we are considering only the conflict of values within the mainstream. For the sake of simplicity we leave out of the picture "outsider" values like the idea that wild nature is more important than human economic welfare.

23. (Paragraph 137) Self-interest is not necessarily MATERIAL self-interest. It can consist in fulfillment of some psychological need, for example, by promoting one's own ideology or religion.

24. (Paragraph 139) A qualification: It is in the interest of the system to permit a certain prescribed degree of freedom in some areas. For example, economic freedom (with suitable limitations and restraints) has proved effective in promoting economic growth. But only planned, circumscribed, limited freedom is in the interest of the system. The individual must always be kept on a leash, even if the leash is sometimes long (see paragraphs 94, 97).

25. (Paragraph 143) We don't mean to suggest that the efficiency or the potential for survival of a society has always been inversely proportional to the amount of pressure or discomfort to which the society subjects people. That certainly is not the case. There is good reason to believe that many primitive societies subjected people to less pressure than European society did, but European society proved far more efficient than any primitive society and always won out in conflicts with such societies because of the advantages conferred by technology.

26. (Paragraph 147) If you think that more effective law enforcement is unequivocally good because it suppresses crime, then remember that crime as defined by the system is not necessarily what YOU would call crime. Today, smoking marijuana is a "crime," and, in some places in the U.S., so is possession of an unregistered handgun. Tomorrow, possession of ANY firearm, registered or not, may be made a crime, and the same thing may happen with disapproved methods of child-rearing, such as spanking. In some countries, expression of dissident political opinions is a crime, and there is no certainty that this will never happen in the U.S., since no constitution or political system lasts forever.

If a society needs a large, powerful law enforcement establishment, then there is something gravely wrong with that society; it must be subjecting people to severe pressures if so many refuse to follow the rules, or follow them only because forced. Many societies in the past have gotten by with little or no formal law-enforcement.

27. (Paragraph 151) To be sure, past societies have had means of influencing human behavior, but these have been primitive and of low effectiveness compared with the technological means that are now being developed.

28. (Paragraph 152) However, some psychologists have publicly expressed opinions indicating their contempt for human freedom. And the mathematician Claude Shannon was quoted in Omni (August 1987) as saying, "I visualize a time when we will be to robots what dogs are to humans, and I'm rooting for the machines."

29. (Paragraph 154) This is no science fiction! After writing paragraph 154 we came across an article in Scientific American according to which scientists are actively developing techniques for identifying possible future criminals and for treating them by a combination of biological and psychological means. Some scientists advocate compulsory application of the treatment, which may be available in the near future. (See "Seeking the Criminal Element," by W. Wayt Gibbs, Scientific American, March 1995.) Maybe you think this is OK because the treatment would be applied to those who might become violent criminals. But of course it won't stop there. Next, a treatment will be applied to those who might become drunk drivers (they endanger human life too), then perhaps to peel who spank their children, then to environmentalists who sabotage logging equipment, eventually to anyone whose behavior is inconvenient for the system.

30. (Paragraph 184) A further advantage of nature as a counter-ideal to technology is that, in many people, nature inspires the kind of reverence that is associated with religion, so that nature could perhaps be idealized on a religious basis. It is true that in many societies religion has served as a support and justification for the established order, but it is also true that religion has often provided a basis for

rebellion. Thus it may be useful to introduce a religious element into the rebellion against technology, the more so because Western society today has no strong religious foundation. Religion, nowadays either is used as cheap and transparent support for narrow, short-sighted selfishness (some conservatives use it this way), or even is cynically exploited to make easy money (by many evangelists), or has degenerated into crude irrationalism (fundamentalist protestant sects, "cults"), or is simply stagnant (Catholicism, main-line Protestantism). The nearest thing to a strong, widespread, dynamic religion that the West has seen in recent times has been the quasi-religion of leftism, but leftism today is fragmented and has no clear, unified, inspiring goal.

Thus there is a religious vacuum in our society that could perhaps be filled by a religion focused on nature in opposition to technology. But it would be a mistake to try to concoct artificially a religion to fill this role. Such an invented religion would probably be a failure. Take the "Gaia" religion for example. Do its adherents REALLY believe in it or are they just play-acting? If they are just play-acting their religion will be a flop in the end.

It is probably best not to try to introduce religion into the conflict of nature vs. technology unless you REALLY believe in that religion yourself and find that it arouses a deep, strong, genuine response in many other people.

31. (Paragraph 189) Assuming that such a final push occurs. Conceivably the industrial system might be eliminated in a somewhat gradual or piecemeal fashion (see paragraphs 4, 167 and Note 4).

32. (Paragraph 193) It is even conceivable (remotely) that the revolution might consist only of a massive change of attitudes toward technology resulting in a relatively gradual and painless disintegration of the industrial system. But if this happens we'll be very lucky. It's far more probably that the transition to a nontechnological society will be very difficult and full of conflicts and disasters.

33. (Paragraph 195) The economic and technological structure of a society are far more important than its political structure in determining the way the average man lives (see paragraphs 95, 119 and Notes 16, 18).

34. (Paragraph 215) This statement refers to our particular brand of anarchism. A wide variety of social attitudes have been called "anarchist," and it may be that many who consider themselves anarchists would not accept our statement of paragraph 215. It should be noted, by the way, that there is a nonviolent anarchist movement whose members probably would not accept FC as anarchist and certainly would not approve of FC's violent methods.

35. (Paragraph 219) Many leftists are motivated also by hostility, but the hostility probably results in part from a frustrated need for power.

36. (Paragraph 229) It is important to understand that we mean someone who sympathizes with these MOVEMENTS as they exist today in our society. One who believes that women, homosexuals, etc., should have equal rights is not necessary a leftist. The feminist, gay rights, etc., movements that exist in our society have the particular ideological tone that characterizes leftism, and if one believes, for example, that women should have equal rights it does not necessarily follow that one must sympathize with the feminist movement as it exists today.

If copyright problems make it impossible for this long quotation to be printed, then please change Note 16 to read as follows:

16. (Paragraph 95) When the American colonies were under British rule there were fewer and less effective legal guarantees of freedom than there were after the American Constitution went into effect, yet there was more personal freedom in pre-industrial America, both before and after the War of Independence, than there was after the Industrial Revolution took hold in this country. In "Violence in America: Historical and Comparative Perspectives," edited by Hugh Davis Graham and Ted Robert Gurr, Chapter 12 by Roger Lane, it is explained how in pre-industrial America the average person had greater independence and autonomy than he does today, and how the process of industrialization necessarily led to the restriction of personal freedom.

LETTERS

Received from T.K.
12-9-96

VERY SENSITIVE   01-0151

Judy, there is a question you've raised with me a couple of times that I tried to answer as best I could, but I didn't feel that I did a very good job of answering it. Since the issue is one that you seem to find disturbing, I'll try to answer your question more clearly now.

You asked how someone like me, who seems to be sensitive to other people's feelings and not vicious or predatory, could do what I've done. Probably the biggest reason why you find my actions incomprehensible is that you have never experienced sufficiently intense anger and frustration over a long enough period of time. You don't know what it means to be under an immense burden of frustrated anger or how vicious it can make one.

Yet there is no inconsistency between viciousness toward those whom one feels are responsible for one's anger, and gentleness toward other people. If anything, having enemies augments one's kindly feelings toward those whom one regards as friends or as fellow victims.

I want to make it clear that I am offering these remarks not as justification but only as explanation. I don't expect you to feel that my actions were justified.

Do *I* feel that my actions were justified? To that I can give you only a qualified yes. My feelings at a given time depend in part on whether I am winning or losing. When I am losing (for example now, when the system has me in jail). I have no doubts or regrets about the means that I've used to fight the system. But when I feel that I'm winning (for example, between the time when the manifesto was published and the time of my arrest), I start feeling sorry for my adversaries, and then I have mixed emotions about what I've done.

Thomas Mosser, for instance, was a practitioner of what I consider to be the slimy technique of public relations, which corporations and other large organizations use to manipulate public opinion, but it does not necessarily follow that he was ill-intentioned. He may simply have felt that the system as it exists today is inevitable, and that he could accomplish nothing by going into another line of work. And of course his death hurt his wife and children, too.

So I can't blame you for feeling troubled about what I've done. In fact, I respect you the more because you have raised this difficult question, even though it makes me uncomfortable to try to answer it. I suppose that to sympathize with my actions one has to hate the system as I hate it, or at least one has to have experienced the kind of prolonged, frustrated anger that I've experienced. I think you have the good fortune never to have gone through anything like that.

I'm grateful that, in spite of your feelings about my actions, you are working so hard to win my case for me.

VERY SENSITIVE

Not as justification, but only to put things in perspective, I offer the following comment.

During the latest U.S. invasion of Panama at least 300 civilians (some say 1,000 or more) were killed through the actions of the U.S. forces. Yet, as far as I know, George Bush has never expressed any remorse or even any mixed feelings about ordering the invasion. (He didn't know in advance that civilians were going to be killed, but he must have realized that there would be a very high risk of civilian deaths, since that sort of thing is commonplace in war).

What was George Bush's motive for ordering the invasion? Certainly it was not to topple a nasty dictator, since there are lots of equally nasty two-bit dictators that the U.S. doesn't bother about. Bush claimed his motive was to stop Noriega's participation in drug trafficking, but it seems to be agreed that by the time of the invasion Noriega was no longer of central importance to the drug trade, and obviously this dictator's removal has done nothing to slow the flow of drugs to the U.S.

Speculations as to Bush's real motive include: a desire to gain political advantage by carrying out a successful military operation; or a desire to install in Panama a government favorable to the United States's retention of control over the Canal Zone when the current treaty expires. But I've heard of no plausible motive for the Panama invasion that would justify 300 civilian deaths.

Yet mainstream opinion does not regard Bush's action as criminal. Why? Because his way of killing people is conventionally acceptable in our society.

TED KACZYNSKI   November 1, 2001
    to

U.K.

Dear Professor:
    Thanks for your letter (even though it bears the inauspicious date of October 3 — my brother's birthday). I don't object to word-processed letters.
    I'm not sure what you're looking for from me, since you don't ask any specific questions or raise any specific points that you want me to address. But since you're an expert in Islamic studies, I do have some fairly specific points that I'd like you to address.
    Like a lot of people, I've been wondering (and not only since Sept. 11) about the significance of militant Islam, and in particular about the motivations of the militants. Some of the motivating factors involved are obvious: resistance to modernizatio religious fanaticism, the leaders' drive for power, and "nationalism." ✱ But the relative importance of the various factors, and their exact nature, has been very unclear to me.
    The first thing I read that seemed to throw

✱ I use the word "nationalism", in quotes, because the phenomenon is similar to nationalism, but differs from it in that it involves identification not with a nation but with a religion.

any real light on the subject was an article in
<u>Time Magazine</u>, October 15, 2001, pages 70-71, titled
"Osama's Endgame." This article <u>seems</u> to show that
Osama Bin Laden's motives (whatever he may tell
himself about them) are not primarily religious piety
or resistance to modernity, but rather "nationalism
and the drive for power. If the article can be
believed, Bin Laden wants nuclear weapons and
economic strength for the Islamic world so that
it can become a "great power." In other words
Bin Laden, behind a veneer of piety, just wants
to play the same power-game that states have
played almost since the beginning of civilization.
It's a game that threatens to become
unprecedentedly disastrous, in several respects,
because states now have at their disposal the
increasingly horrible tools of modern technology.

But I don't know how seriously to take the
<u>Time</u> article, because I've learned through my own
experience that the news media are sloppy in their
research and do not hesitate to distort the truth.

So my first question is: Do you think the
article is roughly accurate in its portrayal of
Bin Laden's motives?

Assuming that the article is more-or-less
accurate as to Bin Laden personally, to what
extent can he be taken as representative of
militant Islam as a whole? I don't doubt that
there are a great many militant Muslims for whom

[TJK to 11/1/01]

religious belief is more important than "nationalism" and the drive for worldly power, but I strongly suspect that those for whom worldly power is most important will tend to dominate the movement. Do you agree, or not?

I also wonder about the strength and nature of the resistance to modernity. Assuming that the article mentioned above is correct, it seems clear that Bin Laden and his associates do not reject modern technology and industrialization — since the Islamic world could hardly become a great power without them. Bin Laden et al resist only the social changes that have accompanied modernization, e.g., collapse of traditional values, irreligion, and unbridled hedonism. I think there _is_ significant resistance to modern technology in the Islamic world,[*] but my guess is that the forces of what I've called "nationalism" will easily prevail over any resistance to modern technology.

Do you agree with the foregoing paragraph, or not?

---

[*] It is interesting that I've received a couple of postcards, unsigned but apparently from the same person, bearing postage stamps of the United Arab Emirates and the words, "From Dubai." No other message; but I assume the sender of the cards knew what I stand for and meant to express his support.

Assuming I am right in thinking that the dominant goal of militant Islam (or at least of its most important leaders) is to create an Islamic "great power", and one that is free of the social changes that have accompanied modernization elsewhere, it seems to me that its project is doomed to fail. Creation of a great power would require industrialization; and it would appear that successful, efficient industrialization is incompatible with the existing culture of the Middle East. An attempt to industrialize that region either will fail or will lead to the same kinds of social changes that have accompanied industrialization elsewhere.

Would you comment on the foregoing paragraph?

I would also guess that, even if the leaders were to drop all resistance to modernizing social changes, creation of a fully-developed and efficient industrial economy in the Middle East, still would be exceedingly slow and difficult, because the culture isn't amenable to it and won't change easily. In particular, there is not enough social discipline there — or not enough social discipline of the right kind. Do you agree or disagree?

Even though a fully-developed industrial economy in the Middle East seems unlikely for the foreseeable future, I can well imagine a Middle-Eastern state that as a whole is inefficient and backward, but in which a relatively small, elite minority creates (on a modest scale) an advanced industrial and technological structure within the more backward whole. Maybe some of the Middle Eastern states already are approaching this condition? What do you think about this?

The possible creation of advanced industrial and technological structures in the Middle East worries me exceedingly. I think that what the West is doing with modern technology is criminally reckless. But I also think that the West shows more self-restraint in the use of its (technological and other) power than most other cultures do. In other words, I think most other cultures that to some degree have access to modern technology use it even more recklessly than the West does. (Did you ever ask yourself what some of these Third-World countries are doing with their nuclear waste?) And it seems to me that there is more recklessness in the Middle East than elsewhere. The danger lies not only in the reckless use of intentionally destructive technologies such as that of nuclear weapons, but also in supposedly benign applications of technologies (e.g., genetic engineering) that may have unanticipated, disastrous consequences. What do you think? Am I right in believing that there is a certain kind of recklessness in Middle-Eastern cultures?

Twenty-odd years ago I worked in a small factory with a man from Pakistan. He was very intelligent, an excellent worker, and I liked him very well. But by way of a joke he used to point a knife at me — a box-cutter knife, as it happened — and say, "I weel keel you!" He apparently did not realize that that kind of humor was not acceptable in the West.

    This is only an anecdote, but it illustrates what I think other evidence seems to support — that in Middle Eastern cultures there is far less inhibition about violence, killing, and destructiveness generally than there is in the West. Am I right about this?

*　　*　　*

    Now let me return to your letter. Your fourth paragraph is obscure to me. Do you mean that you formerly opposed loss of human life but are now more ready to accept it? Or vice versa? You indicate that the deaths at the World Trade Center have affected you more deeply than violent deaths elsewhere in the world. Is this because you see the W.T.C. people as more like yourself, so that you can identify more closely with them? You ask whether that makes you a racist. Whether you call yourself a racist is up to you, but personally I think the leftists' use of the word racist is absurd. If the term is to be applied as broadly as the leftists apply it, then probably 99.9% of people throughout the world's history have been racists.

Also, I'm highly skeptical of the claim that "deaths of innocents occur every day in hundreds of thousand [sic] through the depredations of imperialism." Where I've had opportunity to compare information from leftists with information from sources that I have good reason to believe are reliable, I've found the leftists' information to be shamelessly slanted. (Same true of information from the right.) And, assuming that that statistic ("hundreds of thousands of deaths") were correct, how would your leftist friends balance those deaths against the lives saved by Western medicines and medical technology, Western agricultural technology, etc.? (Not that I think that's good. If I could, I would eliminate all advanced technology everywhere, including medical and agricultural technology.)

And why would you run a support group for I.R.A. prisoners? I certainly can't claim to be well-informed about Northern Ireland, but from the little I know it seems to me that what is going on there is essentially just a blood-feud between the Catholics and the Protestants, and I see no reason why any outsider should think that one side was better than the other.

Sincerely yours,

Ted Kaczynski

You write: "We have noticed that seemingly insignificant individuals are able to garner huge audiences (on the Internet and/or YouTube[*]) for expressing their views, singing, or entertaining others. These ideas often go 'viral' in a matter of minutes, but they are seldom intellectual ideas."

It sounds as if the phenomena you refer to are what sociologists call "fads" or "crazes". Fads and crazes are briefly discussed in the Encyclopaedia Britannica article "Collective Behavior" (15th ed., 2003, Vol. 16, pages 558-59), and are discussed at much greater length by Neil J. Smelser, Theory of Collective Behavior, Macmillan, New York, 1971. Fads and crazes are usually harmless and ephemeral phenomena that serve only to entertain the people who participate in them. Fads and crazes can occasionally have dangerous consequences (e.g., the antisemitic outburst mentioned in the Britannica article), but with its powers of propaganda and of physical coercion the technoindustrial system seems to be consistently able to prevent these occurrences from getting out of hand. Moreover, even if a fad or a craze did totally escape the system's restraints

---

[*] I have no idea what YouTube is.

About Obama... it's interesting that you worked on his campaign. I at first favored Hillary Clinton for president, but after she was out of the picture I favored Obama. I mean, I don't think _any_ of our politicians are worth a damn, so when I say I "favor" a politician for an office, I just mean that I think he or she is the least of the available evils. I favored Clinton and later Obama mainly because I figured a Democratic president would be much more likely than a Republican to appoint judges and Supreme Court Justices who have some respect for constitutional rights. (From my own experiences with the judicial system I know how important that is!) But now I'm afraid Obama is going to be a big disappointment in that respect. The people he has appointed as Attorney

---

TJK to LYDIA ECCLES 4/16/09   2

General and Solicitor General both say they think the government should be able to hold alleged terrorists indefinitely without trial. Of course, the government can _claim_ that anyone is a terrorist, and if there is no trial that claim is never tested. So in effect the government would be abl to lock up _anyone_ indefinitely.

Thus, on the basis of Obama's choices for Attorney General and Solicitor General, I don't think there is any reason to hope that he will appoint good judges.

About my composition -- yes you're right,